SPECTRUM®

Phonics

Grade 2

Spectrum®

An imprint of Carson Dellosa Education
Greensboro, North Carolina

Spectrum®
An imprint of Carson Dellosa Education
P.O. Box 35665
Greensboro, NC 27425 USA

ISBN 978-1-4838-1183-3

02-272207784

Table of Contents

Index of Skills

Phonics Grade 2

Numerals indicate the exercise pages on which these skills appear.

Name _____

Review: Beginning and Ending Sounds

Directions: Say the name of each picture. Write the missing letter or letters to complete each word.

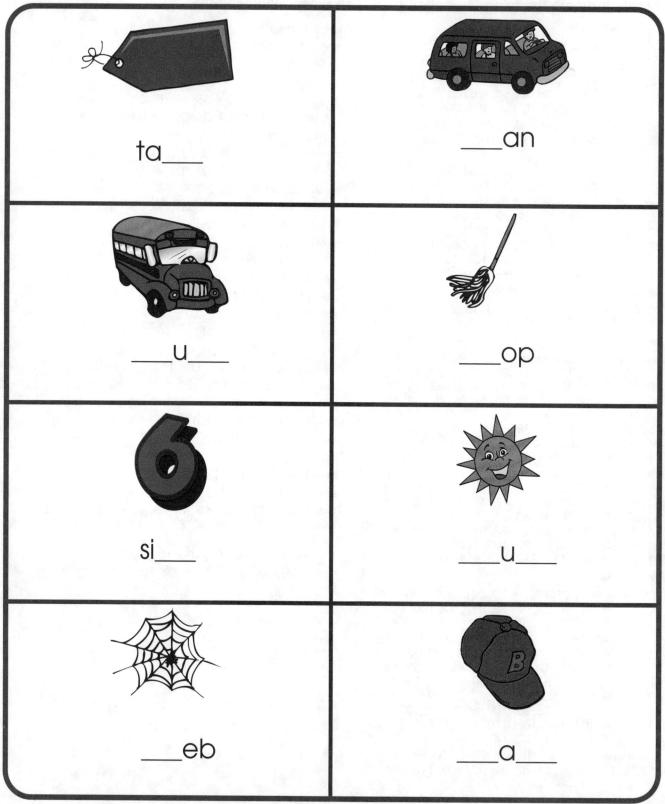

ta____   ____an

____u____   ____op

si____   ____u____

____eb   ____a____

Name _____

Review: Beginning and Ending Sounds

Directions: Say the name of each picture. Write the missing letter or letters to complete each word.

___an

___a___

do___

___i___

___op

be___

___a___

___a___

Name

Short a

Directions: Connect all the pictures whose names have the short **a** sound from the cat to the bag.

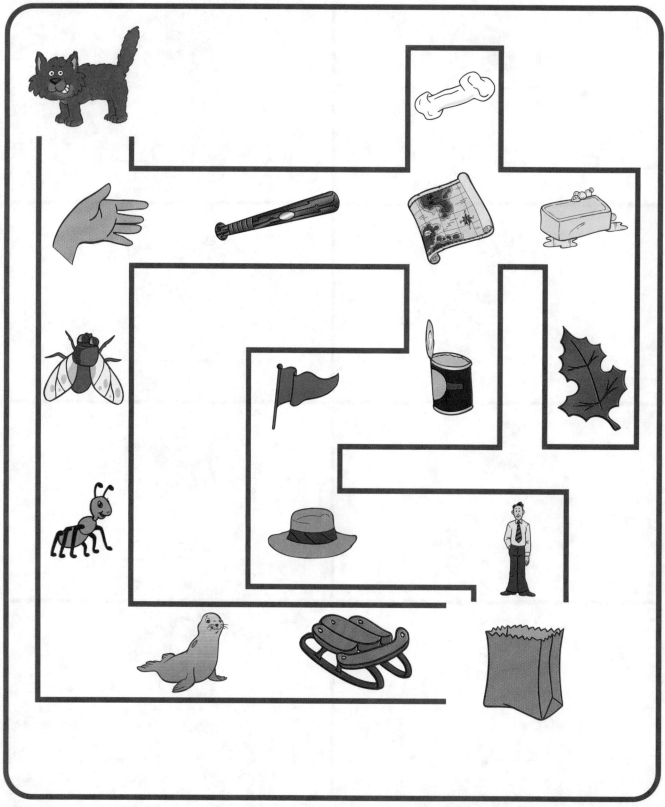

Name _____

Short a

Directions: Write the word from the Word Box that names each picture.

| van | cab | hat | apple | map | pan |
| add | ham | ant | can | hand | ax |

_____

_____

_____

_____

$4+1=5$

_____

_____

_____

_____

Short a

Directions: Write the word from the Word Box that best completes each sentence.

pan   hand   hat   has   ant   as   ham   apple   am

1. An _____ is very tiny.

2. Can you _____ Dad the bag?

3. I wear a _____.

4. I _____ glad.

5. He is _____ tall as a yardstick.

6. Mom will fry fish in a _____.

7. We had _____ for lunch.

8. She _____ a new hat.

9. The _____ is red.

Short e

Directions: Write the word from the Word Box that names each picture.

desk	bed	net	tent	web	leg
nest	hen	egg	jet	belt	dress

_____   _____   _____

_____   _____   _____

_____   _____   _____

_____   _____   _____

Short e

ons: Write a word that rhymes with each word below.

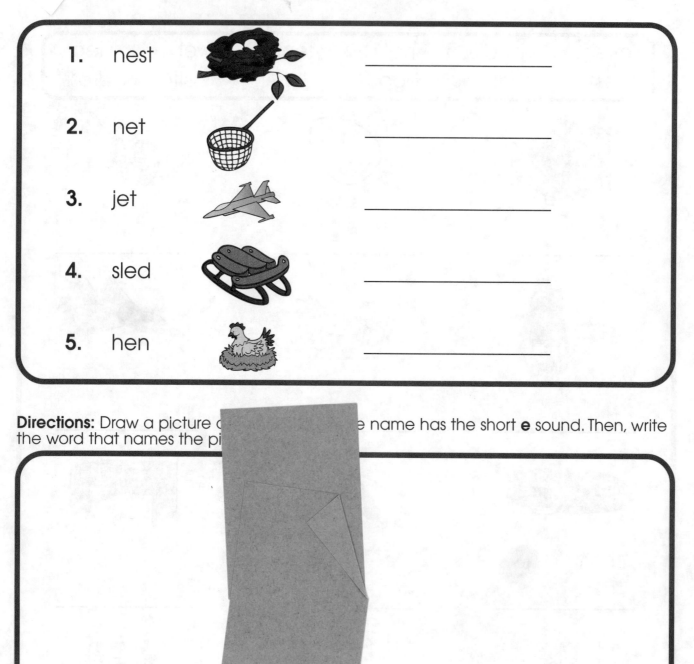

1. nest _____

2. net _____

3. jet _____

4. sled _____

5. hen _____

Directions: Draw a picture ... e name has the short **e** sound. Then, write
the word that names the pi...

_____

Short e

Directions: Write the word from the Word Box that best completes each sentence.

beg	smell	net	wet	nest

1. Dad had the frog in a _____.

2. The bird sleeps in its _____.

3. Can you _____ the flower?

4. The shirt is _____.

5. My dog likes to _____.

Directions: Write two short **e** words of your own. Then, use each word in a sentence.

1. _____   2. _____

1. _____

2. _____

Short i

Directions: Write the word from the Word Box that names each picture.

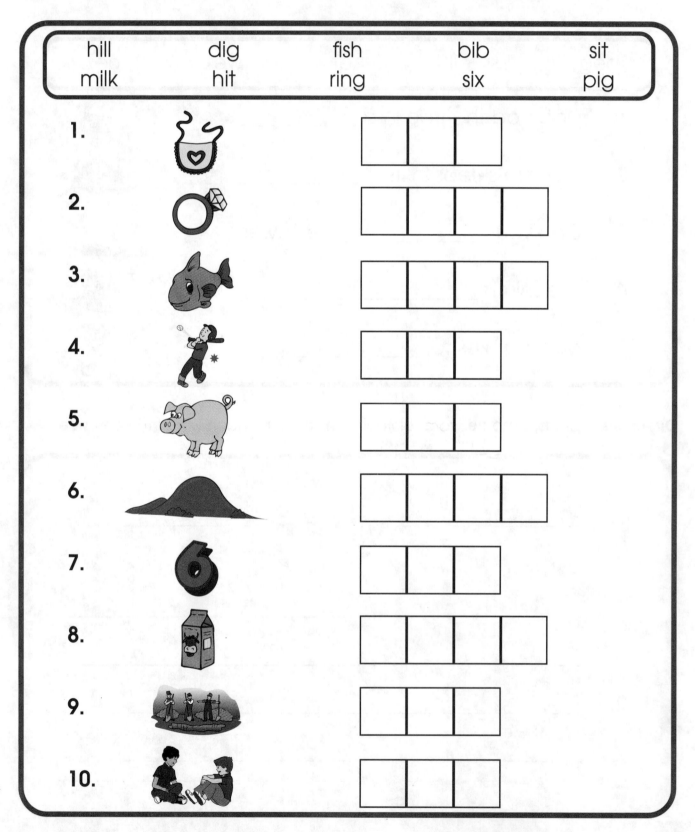

hill	dig	fish	bib	sit
milk	hit	ring	six	pig

1.

2.

3.

4.

5.

6.

7.

8.

9.

10.

Short i

Directions: Write the word from the Word Box that best completes each sentence.

| lid | zip | dig | milk | crib |

1. Spike likes to _____ in the yard.

2. Mom put the baby in the _____.

3. We drink _____ at lunch.

4. Tammy put the _____ on the pan.

5. I can _____ my coat.

Directions: Draw a picture of something whose name has the short **i** sound. Then, write a sentence that tells about your picture.

_____

_____

Short i

Directions: Draw a picture of something that rhymes with each word below. Then, write the rhyming word.

pig   _____

bib   _____

grill   _____

fish   _____

hit   _____

Short o

Directions: Write the word from the Word Box that names each picture.

| dots | cot | lock | cob | box | doll |
| rod | top | pot | hop | fox | mop |

Short o

Directions: Draw a picture of something that rhymes with each word below. Then, write the rhyming word.

box

_____

mop

_____

lock

_____

spot

_____

frog

_____

Short o

Directions: Write the word from the Word Box that best completes each sentence.

hop	top	cot	hot	chop

1.   Molly sleeps on the _____.

2.   Dad can _____ with the ax.

3.   The pot is very _____.

4.   The bunny likes to _____.

5.   Can you spin a _____?

Directions: Draw a picture of something whose name has the short **o** sound. Then, write a sentence that tells about your picture.

_____

_____

Name

Short u

Directions: Write the word from the Word Box that names each picture.

run	cub	pup	tub	nut	sun
bus	mug	hug	bug	bun	rug

Short u

Directions: Draw a picture of something that rhymes with each word below. Then, write the rhyming word.

bun _____

jump _____

hug _____

cub _____

pup _____

Short u

Directions: Write the word from the Word Box that best completes each sentence.

bus	drum	sun	rug	bug

1. The _____ is very hot.

2. I take the _____ to school.

3. I see a _____ on my leg.

4. The _____ is red and white.

5. I can play the _____.

Directions: Draw a picture of something whose name has the short **u** sound. Then, write the word that names the picture.

_____

Name _____

Review: Short Vowels

Directions: Write a vowel in the middle of each puzzle that will make a word across and down.

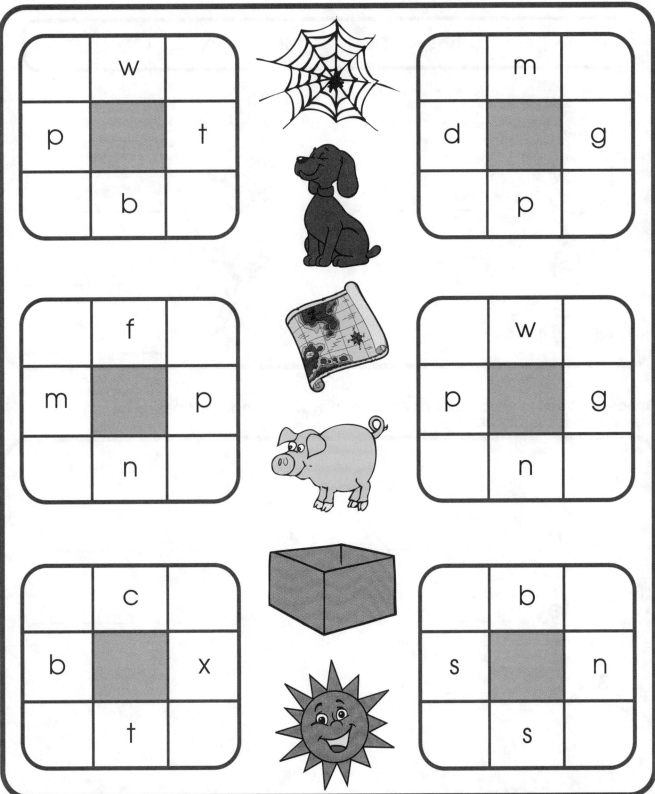

Check Up: Short Vowels

Directions: Write the word from the Word Box that names each picture.

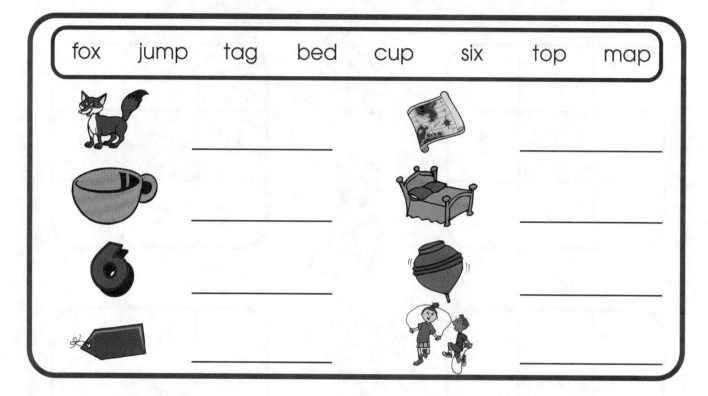

| fox | jump | tag | bed | cup | six | top | map |

Directions: Write a word that has each short vowel sound listed below. Use different words than those above.

1. a _____

2. e _____

3. i _____

4. o _____

5. u _____

Name _____

Long a

Directions: Circle each picture that has the long **a** sound.

Directions: Fill in the missing letters **a** and **e** for each word. Then, write each word again.

1. r___k___ _____

2. c___p___ _____

3. s___f___ _____

4. v___s___ _____

5. c___n___ _____

Long a

Directions: Draw a picture of something that has the long **a** sound. Then, write a sentence that tells about your picture.

_____

_____

Directions: Write the word from the Word Box that best completes each sentence.

ape	lake	cane	vase	bake	game

1. We swim in the _____.

2. Mom put flowers in the _____.

3. Sam plays a _____.

4. I will _____ a cake.

5. Grandpa needs a _____ to walk.

6. We saw an _____ at the zoo.

Name _____

Long i

Directions: Draw a line to match each picture with its name.

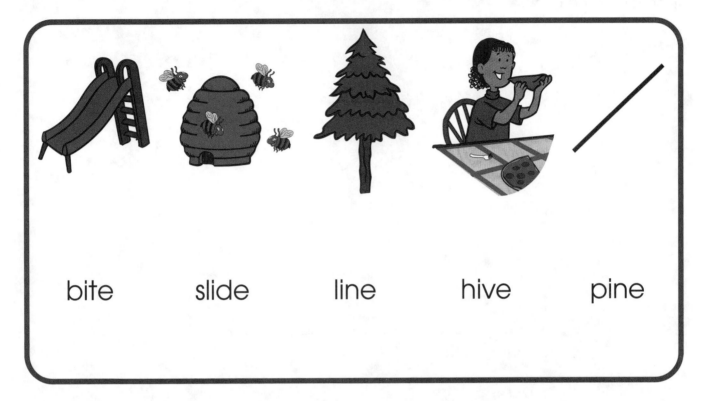

bite   slide   line   hive   pine

Directions: Write the missing letters **i** and **e** for each word. Then, write each word again.

1.   f___v___   _____

2.   v___n___   _____

3.   k___t___   _____

4.   b___k___   _____

Long i

Directions: Draw a picture of something that has the long **i** sound. Then, write the word that names the picture.

_____

Directions: Write the word from the Word Box that best completes each sentence.

| bite | dive | kite | ride | bike | pine |

1. My _____ is up in the tree.

2. I ride my _____ to school.

3. I like the smell of _____ trees.

4. Can you _____ a horse?

5. Take a _____ of the pizza.

6. Dave will _____ into the pool.

Long o

Directions: Write the word from the Word Box that names each picture.

stove	cone	pole	rope	bone	nose

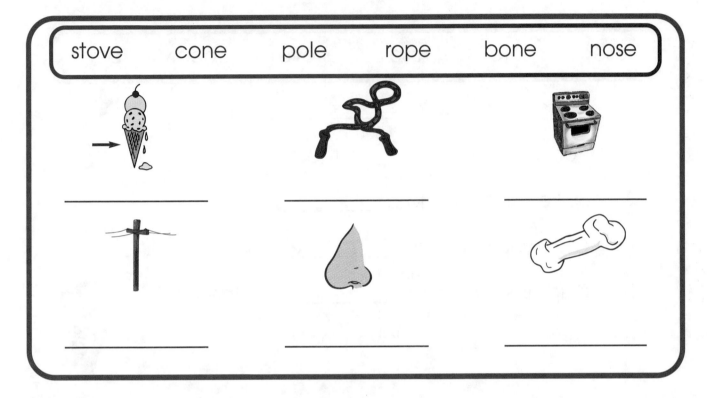

_____   _____   _____

_____   _____   _____

Directions: Write the missing letters **o** and **e** for each word. Then, write each word again.

1.   r____s____   _____

2.   gl____b____   _____

3.   h____s____   _____

Long o

Directions: Write the word from the Word Box that best completes each sentence.

hose	note	rose	stove	rope	bone

1. Mom gave Dad a _____.

2. Put the _____ in the car.

3. Spike will give Fido a _____.

4. Can you sing that _____?

5. Dad has a green _____ in the yard.

6. The _____ is very hot.

Directions: Write the word that names each picture below.

_____   _____   _____

Long u

Directions: Write the missing letters **u** and **e** for each word. Then, write each word again.

1. t___n___   _____

2. m___l___   _____

3. d___n___   _____

4. c___t___   _____

5. c___b___   _____

Directions: Write a word that rhymes with each word below.

1. tube   _____

2. prune   _____

3. flute   _____

Long u

Directions: Circle the word that names the picture. Then, write the word on the line.

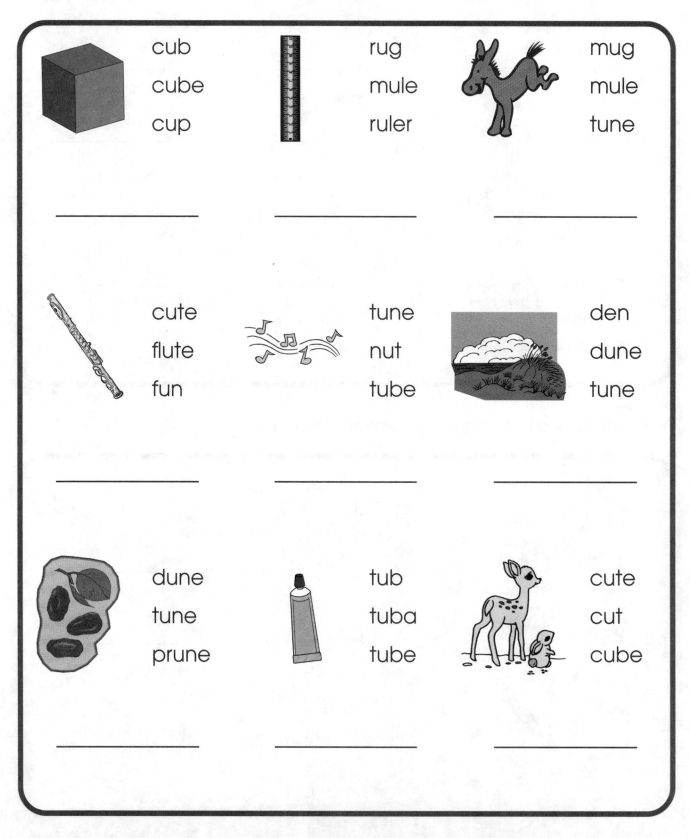

cub
cube
cup

_____

rug
mule
ruler

_____

mug
mule
tune

_____

cute
flute
fun

_____

tune
nut
tube

_____

den
dune
tune

_____

dune
tune
prune

_____

tub
tuba
tube

_____

cute
cut
cube

_____

Name _____

Review: Long Vowels

Directions: Write the missing vowels to complete each word.

1. r___k___

2. r___b___

3. t___p___

4. t___b___

5. k___t___

Directions: Write a word that rhymes with each word below.

1. vine _____

2. gate _____

3. hose _____

4. cube _____

5. wave _____

6. like _____

7. tune _____

8. game _____

Check Up: Long Vowels

Directions: Write the word from the Word Box that names each picture.

cape	safe	bike	vase	mule	bone
tube	prune	hose	cone	cube	nine

Name _____

Short and Long Vowels

Directions: Write the word from the Word Box that names each picture.

duck   pan   rod   skates   lips   tape
cub   dress   slide   cone   vine   flute

Short and Long Vowels

Directions: Write each picture name in the correct column.

Short Vowel Words

_____

_____

_____

_____

_____

_____

Long Vowel Words

_____

_____

_____

_____

_____

_____

Short and Long Vowels

Directions: Write the missing vowel or vowels for each word.

1. b___g

2. b___k___

3. r___p___

4. b___d

5. n___s___

6. t___p

7. m___p

8. m___l___

9. b___b

10. p___n___

Short and Long Vowels

Directions: Draw a picture of something whose name has the vowel sound written in each box. Then, write the word that names each picture.

Long u	Short a	Short e
_____	_____	_____
Long i	**Long o**	**Short i**
_____	_____	_____
Short u	**Long a**	**Short o**
_____	_____	_____

Check Up: Short and Long Vowels

Directions: Circle the word that best completes each sentence. Then, write the word in the blank.

1. Lisa put the hat in the _____.
   bone   box   robe

2. A _____ is a very large animal.
   hag   hose   hog

3. The mother bear takes care of her _____.
   cube   cup   cub

4. Let's play a _____.
   gum   gate   game

5. I will play a _____ on the flute.
   tub   tube   tune

6. Put the _____ on the boat.
   robe   rope   nine

7. I like to go down the _____.
   five   fish   slide

8. He will wash the dog in the _____.
   tub   tube   tag

Name _____

Hard and Soft c

Directions: The letter **c** can have the hard sound of **k**. It can also have the soft sound of **s**. Draw a line to match each word with its picture.

Hard **c** = calf   Soft **c** = cent

cot   ice   city   coat

Directions: Write each picture name from above in the correct column.

Hard c Words   Soft c Words

_____   _____

_____   _____

Name _____

Hard and Soft c

Directions: Write the word from the Word Box that names each picture.

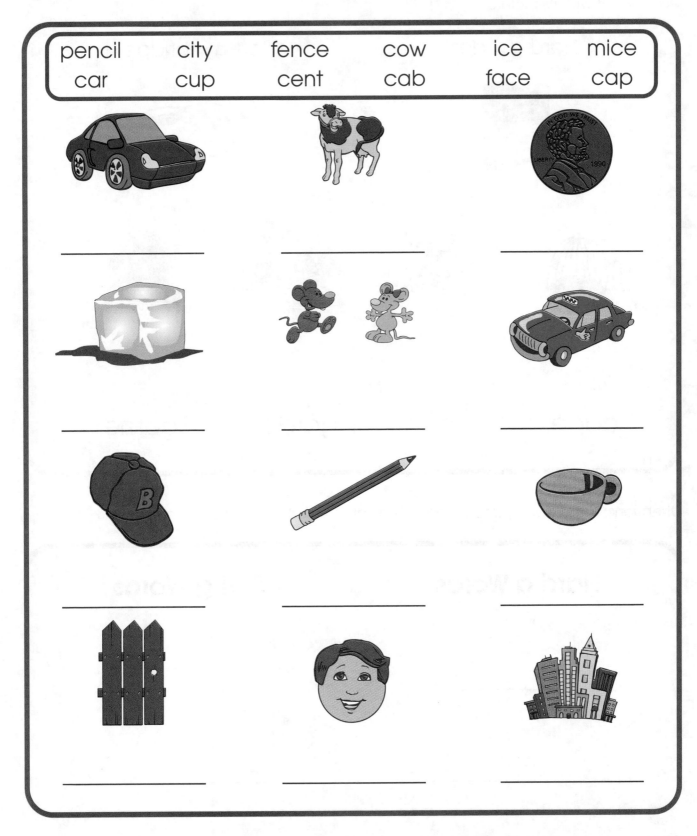

pencil   city   fence   cow   ice   mice
car   cup   cent   cab   face   cap

Hard and Soft g

Directions: The letter **g** can have a hard sound and a soft sound. Draw a line to match each word with its picture.

Hard **g** = gas   Soft **g** = bridge

cage   stage   garden   game

Directions: Write each picture name from above in the correct column.

Hard g Words	**Soft g Words**
_____	_____
_____	_____

Name _____

Hard and Soft g

Directions: Write the word from the Word Box that names each picture.

wig	edge	judge	goat	gate	cage
stage	globe	dog	page	bridge	pig

Review: Hard and Soft c and g

Directions: Write the missing letter **c** or **g** for each word. Then, circle the word hard or soft to tell how the letter sounds.

1. ____as hard soft

2. sta____e hard soft

3. ____age hard soft

4. fa____e hard soft

5. i____e hard soft

6. brid____e hard soft

7. ____alf hard soft

8. ____arden hard soft

9. jud____e hard soft

10. mi____e hard soft

Check Up: Hard and Soft c and g

Directions: Circle the word that best completes each sentence. Then, write the word in the blank.

1. Mom has on a _____ dress.
    leg   lace   place

2. We will drive across the _____.
    judge   fence   bridge

3. We saw a _____ at the farm.
    goat   gas   edge

4. Dad goes to work in the _____.
    ice   fence   city

5. Emily wears a _____ when it is cold.
    cow   cab   coat

6. What do you plant in your _____?
    cup   cage   garden

7. Mom does not like _____.
    edge   mice   pencil

8. The _____ is a kind man.
    judge   page   cent

Consonant Blends With S

Directions: Write the consonant blend that shows the beginning sound of each picture name.

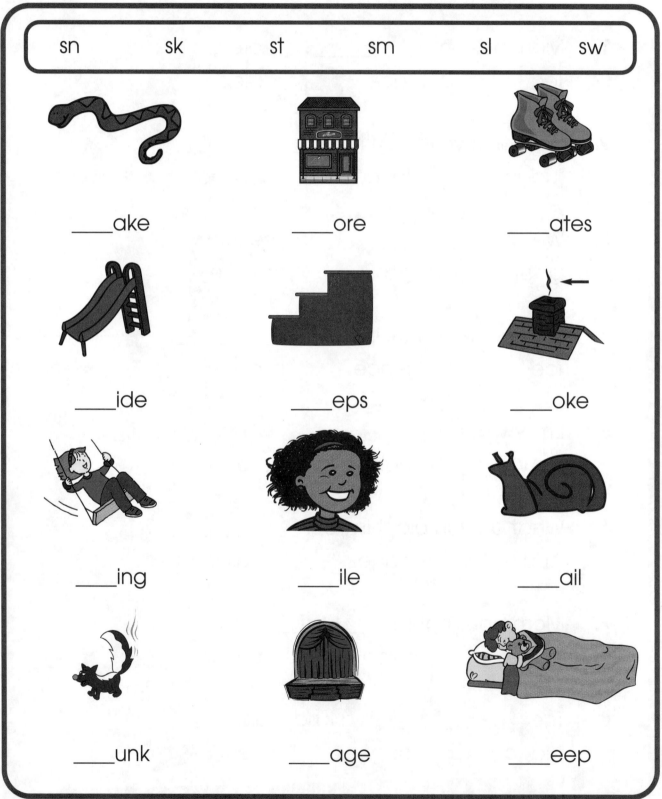

| sn | sk | st | sm | sl | sw |

___ake

___ore

___ates

___ide

___eps

___oke

___ing

___ile

___ail

___unk

___age

___eep

Consonant Blends With S

Directions: Write the word from the Word Box that names each picture.

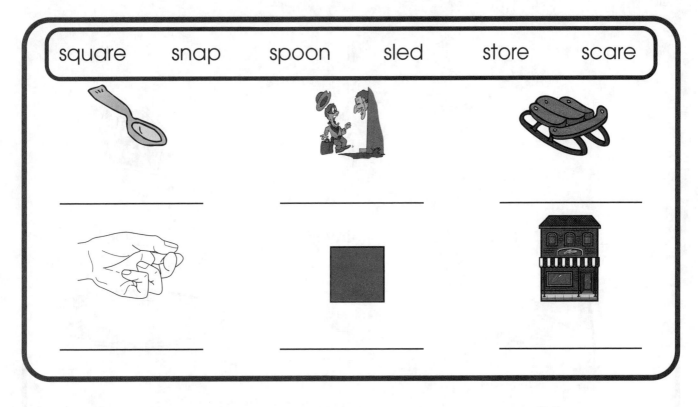

square	snap	spoon	sled	store	scare

_____   _____   _____

_____   _____   _____

Directions: Write two sentences. Use one word from above in each sentence.

1. _____

   _____

2. _____

   _____

Consonant Blends With L

Directions: Write the consonant blend that shows the beginning sound of each picture name.

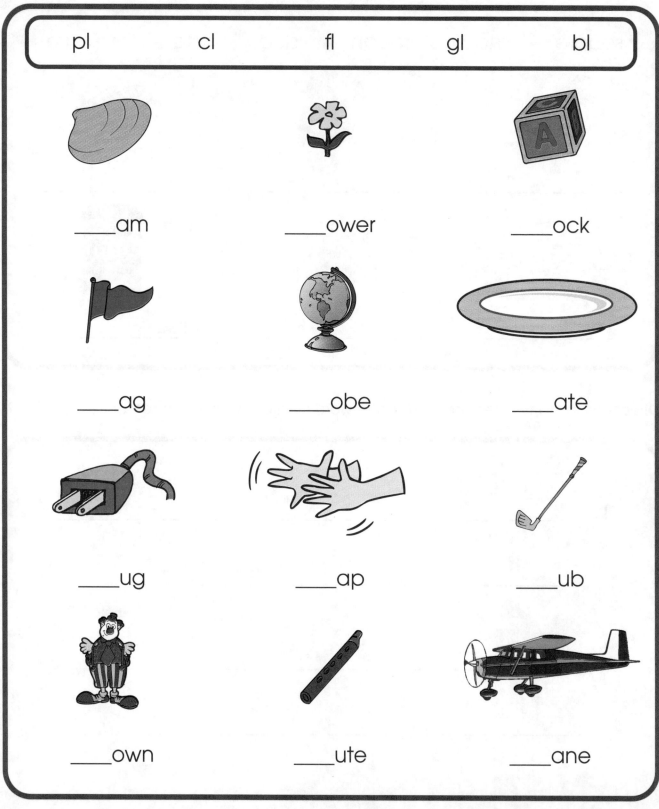

pl   cl   fl   gl   bl

___am   ___ower   ___ock

___ag   ___obe   ___ate

___ug   ___ap   ___ub

___own   ___ute   ___ane

Consonant Blends With L

Directions: Write the word from the Word Box that names each picture.

blow	clip	flame	glass	fly	flute

_____ _____ _____

_____ _____ _____

Directions: Write two sentences. Use one word from above in each sentence.

1. _____

   _____

2. _____

   _____

Consonant Blends With R

Directions: Write the consonant blend that shows the beginning sound of each picture name.

dr   br   cr   fr   tr   pr

___ide   ___og   ___ow

___idge   ___ab   ___ess

___um   ___ap   ___ize

___oom   ___ame   ___uit

Consonant Blends With R

Directions: Write the word from the Word Box that names each picture.

crayon	tray	prince	dress	crown	tree

_____   _____   _____

_____   _____   _____

Directions: Write two sentences. Use one word from above in each sentence.

1. _____

   _____

2. _____

   _____

Name _____

Review: Consonant Blends

Directions: Write the word from the Word Box that names each picture.

bridge	stage	snake	grass	tree	crab
crown	sled	globe	flag	plug	bride

_____   _____   _____

_____   _____   _____

_____   _____   _____

_____   _____   _____

Final Consonant Blends

Directions: Write the final consonant blend for each word. Then, write each word again.

1. ca_____   _____

2. de_____   _____

3. roa_____   _____

4. toa_____   _____

5. ma_____   _____

Directions: Write the word that rhymes with each word below.

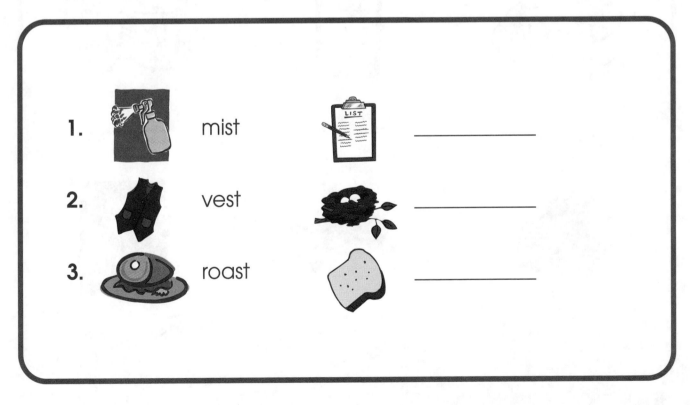

1. mist   _____

2. vest   _____

3. roast   _____

Final Consonant Blends

Directions: Circle the consonant blend that you hear at the end of each picture name.

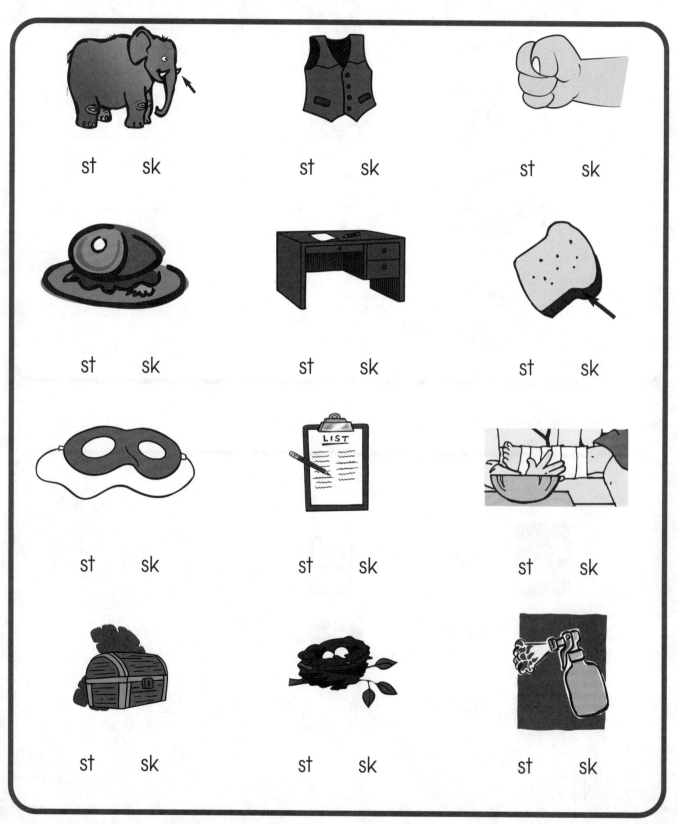

st sk	st sk	st sk
st sk	st sk	st sk
st sk	st sk	st sk
st sk	st sk	st sk

Name _____

Review: Final Consonant Blends

Directions: Write the word from the Word Box that names each picture.

mask   list   vest   desk   fist   mist

chest   tusk   roast   nest   crust   toast

Final Consonant Blends

Directions: Write the final consonant blend of each word. Then, write each word again.

1.   sta_____   _____

2.   pai_____   _____

3.   sku_____   _____

4.   pla_____   _____

5.   ce_____   _____

Directions: Write a word that rhymes with each word below.

1.   band   _____

2.   stump   _____

3.   sink   _____

Final Consonant Blends

Directions: Circle the word that names each picture.

pond
point
paint

bank
crank
cent

stand
cent
tent

pump
paint
plant

lamp
pump
stump

wink
sink
wind

band
bank
pond

ant
stand
and

stump
stamp
stand

stump
pond
pump

Name _____

Review: Final Consonant Blends

Directions: Write the word from the Word Box that names each picture.

| cast | cent | mask | hand | plant | lamp |
| skunk | sink | pond | desk | bank | stamp |

Final Consonant Blends

Directions: Write the final consonant blend to complete each word. Then, write each word again.

1. ra_____ _____

2. qui_____ _____

3. wo_____ _____

4. wi_____ _____

5. go_____ _____

Directions: Write the word that rhymes with each word below.

1. shelf _____

2. lift _____

3. melt _____

Name _____

Final Consonant Blends

Directions: Circle the word that names each picture.

shelf
elf
wolf

melt
belt
self

lift
gift
golf

left
elf
let

craft
lift
raft

melt
shelf
elf

Directions: Write two sentences. Use one word that you circled above in each sentence.

1. _____

   _____

2. _____

   _____

Review: Final Consonant Blends

Directions: Write the word from the Word Box that names each picture.

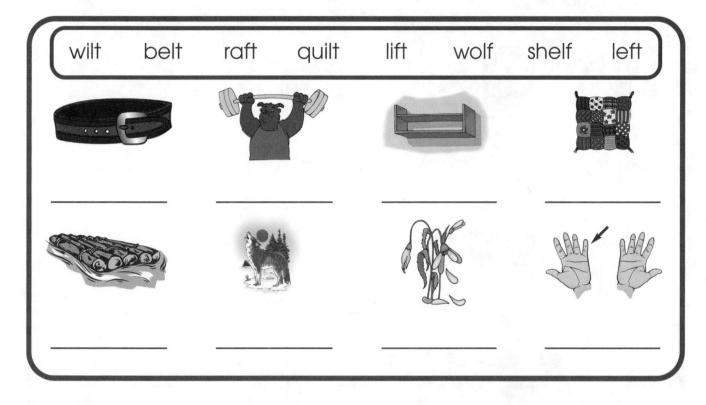

wilt	belt	raft	quilt	lift	wolf	shelf	left

_____   _____   _____   _____

_____   _____   _____   _____

Directions: Look at the picture and write the word that best completes each sentence.

1. The _____ is very small.

2. Mom gave Dad a _____.

3. Do you play _____?

4. Put the books on the _____.

5. The ice will _____ in the sun.

Three-Letter Consonant Blends

Directions: Write a three-letter consonant blend to complete each word. Then, write each word again.

1. _____eet _____

2. _____ew _____

3. _____it _____

4. _____eam _____

5. _____eam _____

6. _____ub _____

7. _____ash _____

8. _____ing _____

9. _____ap _____

10. _____ong _____

Three-Letter Consonant Blends

Directions: Draw a picture to go with each word below. Then, write a sentence that tells about each picture. Make sure to use the word in the sentence.

scream

_____

_____

street

_____

_____

splash

_____

_____

scrub

_____

_____

Three-Letter Consonant Blends

Directions: Write the word from the Word Box that best completes each sentence.

stripes	scrape	street	sprain	scrub
spray	scrap	splash	stream	

1. There are many houses on my _____.

2. Dad will _____ the garden with the hose.

3. Steve makes a big _____ when he jumps in the pool.

4. Write your name on this _____ of paper.

5. Grandpa and I fish in the _____.

6. I do not like to _____ the floor.

7. Oliver has a _____ on his knee.

8. My new kitten has black and gray _____.

9. Mom got a bad _____ when she fell.

Review: 3-Letter Consonant Blends

Directions: Write the word from the Word Box that names each picture.

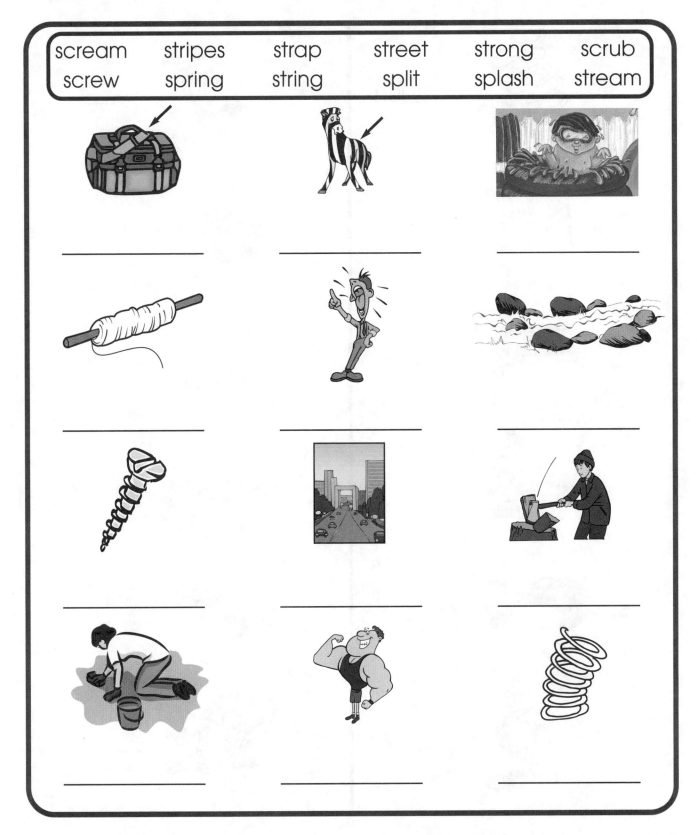

scream	stripes	strap	street	strong	scrub
screw	spring	string	split	splash	stream

Name _____

Check Up: Consonant Blends

Directions: Write a consonant blend to complete each word.

1. ____ing

2. ____ag

3. ____ay

4. ____it

5. de____

6. ____own

7. sku____

8. ne____

9. ____oon

10. ____ake

11. ____idge

12. ____og

Silent Consonants

Directions: Write **kn** or **wr** to show the letters that make the beginning sound of each picture name.

The letters **kn** make the sound of **n**.
The letters **wr** make the sound of **r**.

knife   **wr**ist

____ot   ____ite   ____eath

____ee   ____ock   ____ap

Directions: Write two sentences. Use one word from above in each sentence.

1. _____

   _____

2. _____

   _____

Name _____

Silent Consonants

Directions: Write the word from the Word Box that names each picture.

| wrench | knock | wrist | kneel | write | knit |

_____   _____   _____

_____   _____   _____

Directions: Write two sentences. Use one word from above in each sentence.

1. _____

   _____

2. _____

   _____

Silent Consonants

Directions: Write the word from the Word Box that best completes each sentence.

knot	write	wrap	knife	
know	knock	knee	knit	wrong

1. Can you _____ this gift for Mom?

2. I _____ how to swim.

3. T.J. likes to _____ letters.

4. I fell and hurt my _____.

5. The telephone call was a _____ number.

6. Grandma wants to _____ a scarf for me.

7. There was a _____ in the rope.

8. I hear a _____ at the door.

9. Put a _____ and fork on the table.

Name _____

Silent Consonants

Directions: Write the word from the Word Box that names each picture.

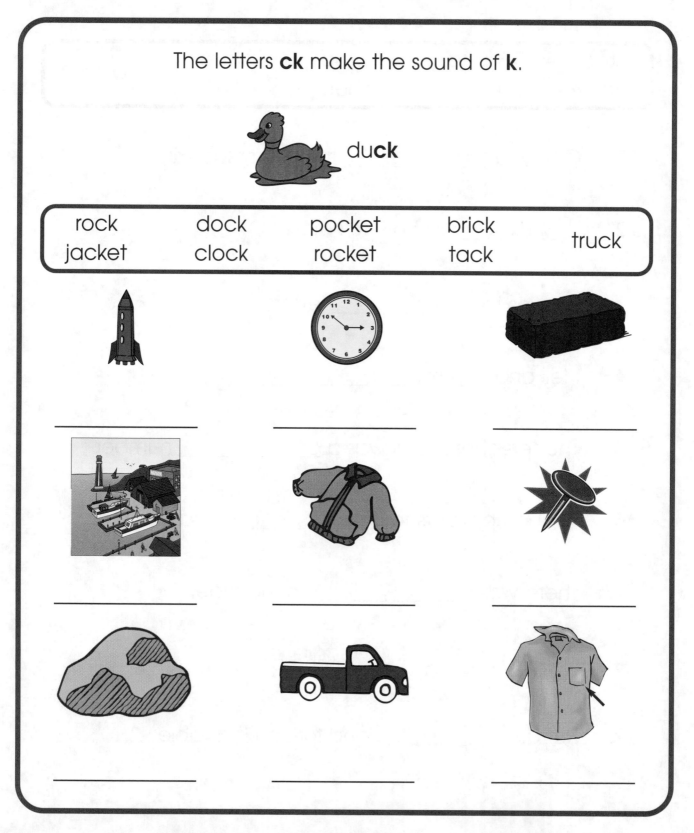

The letters **ck** make the sound of **k**.

du**ck**

rock	dock	pocket	brick	
jacket	clock	rocket	tack	truck

_____ _____ _____

_____ _____ _____

_____ _____ _____

Silent Consonants

Directions: Draw a picture to go with each word below. Then, write a sentence that tells about each picture. Make sure to use the word in the sentence.

pocket	rocket
_____ _____	_____ _____
truck	**rock**
_____ _____	_____ _____

Silent Consonants

Directions: Write the word from the Word Box that best completes each sentence.

pack	duck	snack	chicks	dock
clock	tricks	lock	black	

1. Did you hear that _____ quack?

2. My _____ shows the wrong time.

3. Grandma has baby _____ at the farm.

4. Dad gave me a _____ for my bike.

5. My dog has _____ and white fur.

6. Mom steered the boat to the _____.

7. Dave put his books in his _____.

8. Matt likes to play _____ on his friends.

9. I am hungry for a _____.

Name _____

Silent Consonants

Directions: Write the word from the Word Box that names each picture.

When **g** and **h** are together in a word, they are often silent.

8 ei**gh**t

| eighty | light | knight | high | bright | night |

Directions: Write two sentences. Use one word from above in each sentence.

1. _____

   _____

2. _____

   _____

Silent Consonants

Directions: Write the word from the Word Box that best completes each sentence.

might	right	fight	night	
tight	eighty	light	high	sight

1. Grandpa is almost _____ years old.

2. We _____ not have school tomorrow.

3. My red jacket is too _____.

4. Mom was _____ about the storm.

5. The snowy trees are a pretty _____.

6. The _____ is very bright.

7. It rained all _____ long.

8. I can't reach that _____ shelf.

9. Dad doesn't like it when we _____.

Review: Silent Consonants

Directions: Write a sentence that tells about each picture.

1. _____
   _____

2. _____
   _____

3. _____
   _____

4. _____
   _____

5. _____
   _____

6. _____
   _____

Check Up: Silent Consonants

Directions: Write the word from the Word Box that names each picture.

chicks   rock   lock   knit   knight   knock
wrist   write   pocket   wrap   knot   light

_____   _____   _____

_____   _____   _____

_____   _____   _____

_____   _____   _____

Vowel Pairs: AI and AY

Directions: The vowel pairs **ai** and **ay** can make the long **a** sound. Write the word that rhymes with each word below.

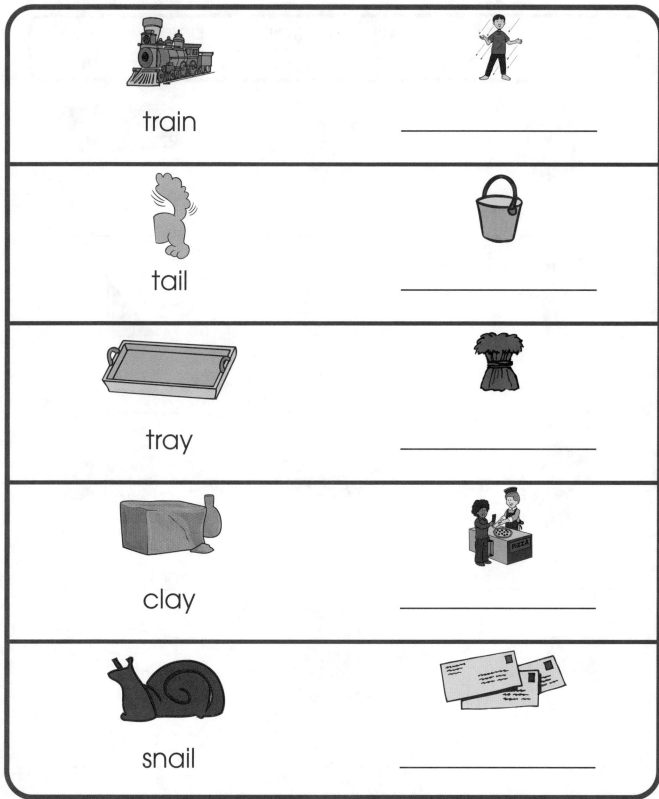

train

_____

tail

_____

tray

_____

clay

_____

snail

_____

Vowel Pairs: AI and AY

Directions: Write the word from the Word Box that names each picture.

clay	pail	tail	train	paint	mail
rain	stain	chain	pay	sail	tray

Vowel Pairs: AI and AY

Directions: Write the word from the Word Box that best completes each sentence.

paint	tray	mail	snail	hay
rain	tail	clay	train	

1. The _____ is in its shell.

2. Dad brought us cookies on a _____.

3. The cows eat _____.

4. Kelly made a bowl from _____.

5. We don't like to play outside in the _____.

6. Fluffy wags his _____ when he is happy.

7. What color _____ should we use?

8. Grandma took the _____ when she came to see us.

9. I bring in the _____ every day.

Vowel Pairs: EE and EA

Directions: The vowel pairs **ee** and **ea** can make the long **e** sound. Write the word from the Word Box that names each picture.

beads	tree	seal	bee	feet	seat

_____   _____   _____

_____   _____   _____

Directions: Write two sentences. Use one word from above in each sentence.

1. _____

   _____

2. _____

   _____

Vowel Pairs: EE and EA

Directions: Draw a picture to go with each word below. Then, write a sentence that tells about each picture. Make sure to use the word in the sentence.

leaf

beach

_____

_____

feet

sleep

_____

_____

Name _____

Vowel Pairs: EE and EA

Directions: The vowel pair **ea** can also make the short **e** sound, as in head. Write the word from the Word Box that best completes each sentence.

bread	leak	steam	beak	sleep
beach	sheep	head	leap	

1. Our kitchen sink has a _____.

2. Do you like to swim at the _____?

3. The frog can _____ over the log.

4. Mom likes to bake wheat _____.

5. The bird has a very sharp _____.

6. A baby _____ is called a lamb.

7. James hit his _____ on the shelf.

8. Ryan and Eric will _____ in the tent tonight.

9. I see _____ coming from the teakettle.

Vowel Pairs: OA and OW

Directions: The vowel pairs **oa** and **ow** can make the long **o** sound. Write the word from the Word Box that names each picture.

pillow	goat	snow	road	crow	soap

_____   _____   _____

_____   _____   _____

Directions: Write two sentences. Use one word from above in each sentence.

1. _____

_____

2. _____

_____

Vowel Pairs: OA and OW

Directions: Draw a picture to go with each word below. Then, write a sentence that tells about each picture. Make sure to use the word in the sentence.

coat	window
_____ _____	_____ _____
bowl	**toad**
_____ _____	_____ _____

Vowel Pairs: OA and OW

Directions: Write the word from the Word Box that best completes each sentence.

toad	row	grown	goat	
bowl	throw	toast	coat	pillow

1. A baby _____ is called a kid.

2. Can you _____ the ball to Amy?

3. I left my new wool _____ at school.

4. Mom gave me a soft _____.

5. That _____ has bumpy skin.

6. Let's make a _____ of popcorn.

7. The baby has _____ a lot in three months.

8. Dad made eggs and _____ for breakfast.

9. We can _____ the boat into the middle of the lake.

Review: Vowel Pairs

Directions: Write the missing vowel pair for each word. Then, write each word again.

1.   b_____k   _____

2.   h_____   _____

3.   s_____p   _____

4.   br_____d   _____

5.   sl_____p   _____

6.   b_____l   _____

7.   s_____l   _____

8.   sn_____l   _____

9.   l_____f   _____

10.   cr_____   _____

Vowel Pair: OO

Directions: The vowel pair **oo** can make a short sound, as in hook, and a long sound, as in moon. Write the word that rhymes with each word below.

spoon   _____

book   _____

spool   _____

wood   _____

stools   _____

Name _____

Vowel Pair: OO

Directions: Write the word from the Word Box that names each picture.

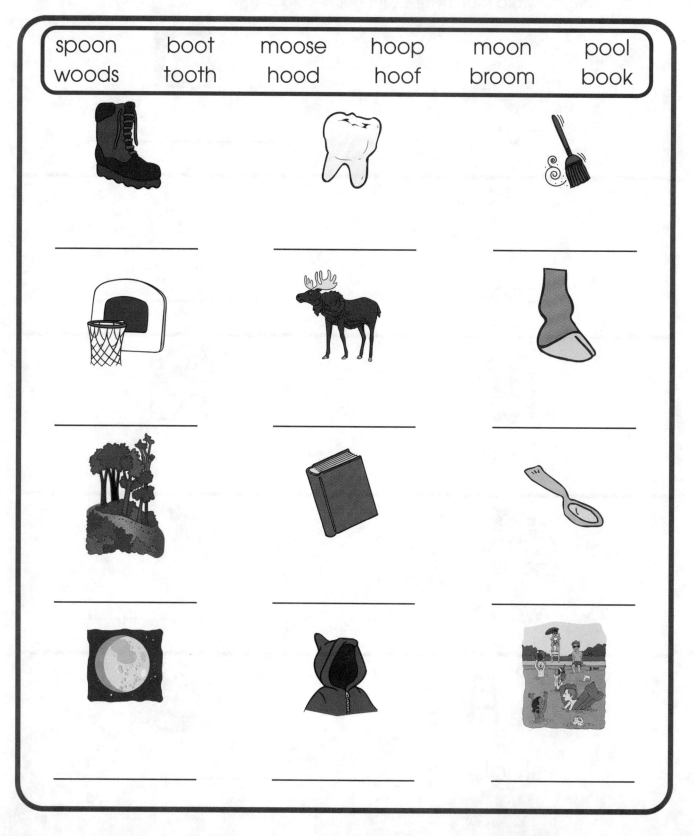

spoon   boot   moose   hoop   moon   pool

woods   tooth   hood   hoof   broom   book

_____   _____   _____

_____   _____   _____

_____   _____   _____

_____   _____   _____

Vowel Pairs: AU and AW

Directions: The vowel pairs **au** and **aw** can make the sound that you hear in the middle of the words cause and lawn. In each row, write the two words that rhyme with the first word in the row.

fawn _____ _____

claw _____ _____

Directions: Draw lines to match the words and pictures.

sauce   laundry   faucet   auto

Vowel Pairs: AU and AW

Directions: Write the word from the Word Box that names each picture.

straw	saw	crawl	fawn	auto	claw
paw	sauce	yawn	faucet	laundry	lawn

_____   _____   _____

_____   _____   _____

_____   _____   _____

Vowel Pairs: AU and AW

Directions: Write the word from the Word Box that best completes each sentence.

fawn	caught	straw	auto	lawn
faucet	crawl	shawl	saw	

1. Dad put a new _____ on the sink.

2. A baby deer is called a _____.

3. Mom cut the wood with a _____.

4. My baby brother is just learning to _____.

5. The fish got _____ in the net.

6. Our family bought a new car at the _____ show.

7. The _____ is nice and green in the spring.

8. Grandma wears a _____ to keep warm.

9. Ryan sips his milk through a _____.

Name _____

Vowel Pair: EW

Directions: The vowel pair **ew** can make the long **u** sound. Write the word from the Word Box that names each picture.

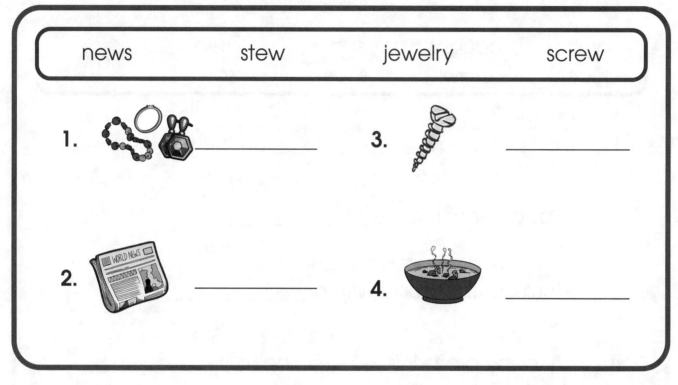

news	stew	jewelry	screw

1. _____

2. _____

3. _____

4. _____

Directions: Write two sentences. Use one word from the Word Box in each sentence.

flew	new	few	grew

1. _____

_____

2. _____

_____

Vowel Pair: EW

Directions: Write the word from the Word Box that best completes each sentence.

chew	grew	dew	jewelry	stew
drew	few	flew	news	

1. Last year, we _____ beans in our garden.

2. We went to the beach a _____ times this summer.

3. There is _____ on the lawn in the morning.

4. Have you heard the good _____?

5. Mom made beef _____ for dinner.

6. Mary _____ a picture of Mom.

7. Murphey likes to _____ on a bone.

8. Mom likes to wear _____.

9. The bird _____ high in the sky.

Name _____

Review: Vowel Pairs

Directions: Write the word from the Word Box that names each picture.

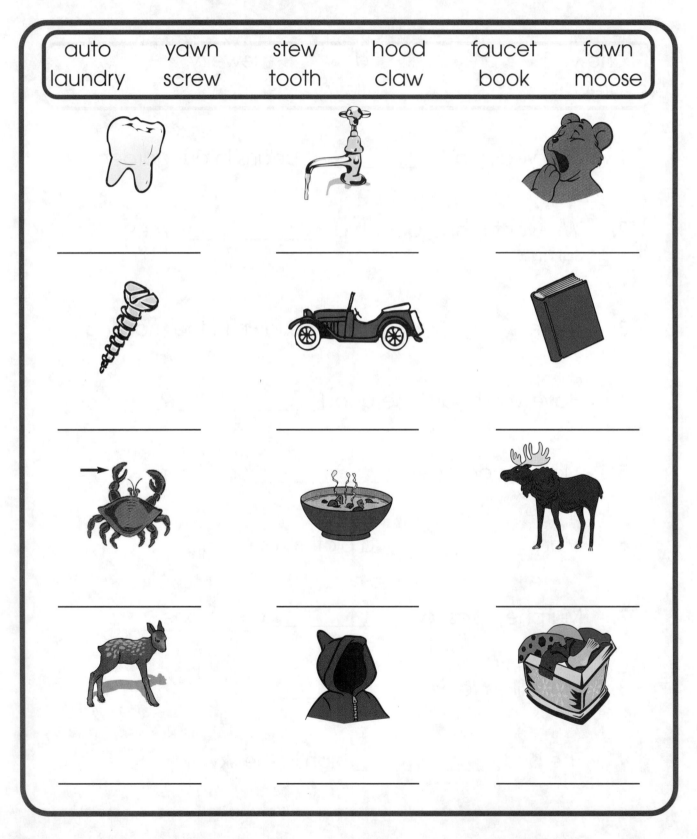

auto	yawn	stew	hood	faucet	fawn
laundry	screw	tooth	claw	book	moose

_____   _____   _____

_____   _____   _____

_____   _____   _____

_____   _____   _____

Name _____

The Sounds of Y

Directions: Read the words. Write each word in the correct column.

Sometimes **y** can sound like long **e**,
and sometimes it can sound like long **i**.

pupp**y**   fr**y**

dry   baby   city   sky

pony   fly   bunny   cry

Y as Long e   **Y as Long i**

_____   _____

_____   _____

_____   _____

_____   _____

The Sounds of Y

Directions: Write the word from the Word Box that names each picture.

bunny	fly	cry	money	muddy	city
puppy	sky	baby	fry	key	dry

_____   _____   _____

_____   _____   _____

_____   _____   _____

_____   _____   _____

The Sounds of Y

Directions: Write the word from the Word Box that best completes each sentence.

silly	cry	city	story	
try	muddy	happy	fry	puppy

1. Can you hear the baby _____?

2. The _____ is a busy place.

3. Dad will _____ not to be late.

4. It is _____ after it rains.

5. My brother takes good care of his new _____.

6. Elise is _____ when she reads.

7. Molly will read us a _____.

8. Josh told us a _____ joke.

9. Do you know how to _____ an egg?

Check Up: Vowel Pairs and Sounds of Y

Directions: Write the name of each picture.

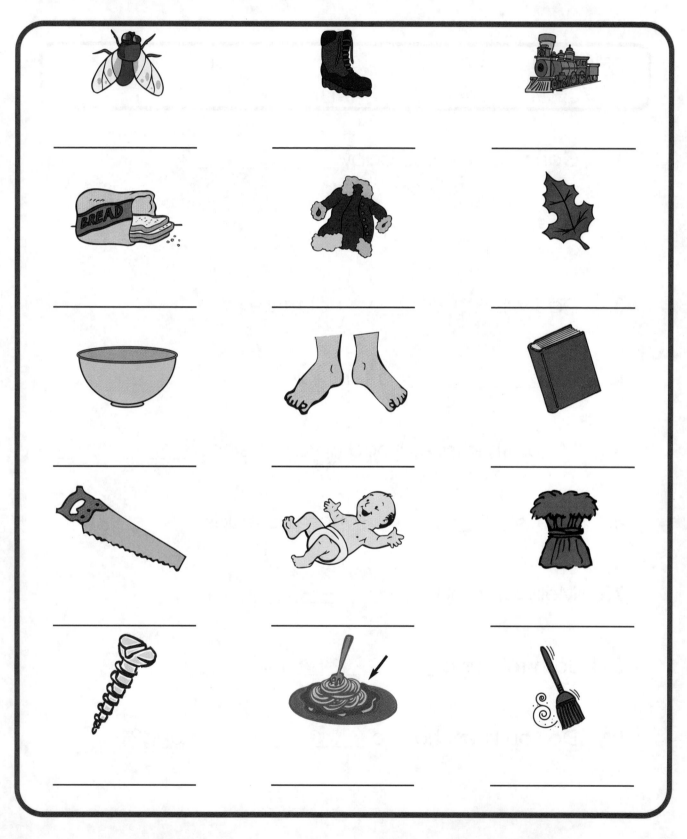

Name _____

Consonant Pairs

Directions: Write the letters **sh**, **ch**, **th**, or **wh** to complete each word. Then, write each word again.

1. _____op   _____

2. _____read   _____

3. _____ell   _____

4. _____ree   _____

5. _____ale   _____

6. _____ain   _____

7. _____in   _____

8. _____icks   _____

9. _____eel   _____

10. _____oe   _____

Name _____

Consonant Pairs

Directions: Write the word from the Word Box that names each picture.

wheel	ship	chair	whale	shoe	shelf
think	cheese	throat	thread	cheek	thin

_____ _____ _____

_____ _____ _____

_____ _____ _____

_____ _____ _____

Final Consonant Pairs

Directions: Write the final consonant pair **sh**, **ch**, **tch**, **th**, or **ng** to complete each word. Then, write each word again.

1. ri____   _____

2. spri____   _____

3. di____   _____

4. bran____   _____

5. chur____   _____

6. stri____   _____

7. ba____   _____

8. bru____   _____

9. wi____   _____

10. too____   _____

Name _____

Final Consonant Pairs and Blends

Directions: Write the word that rhymes with each word below.

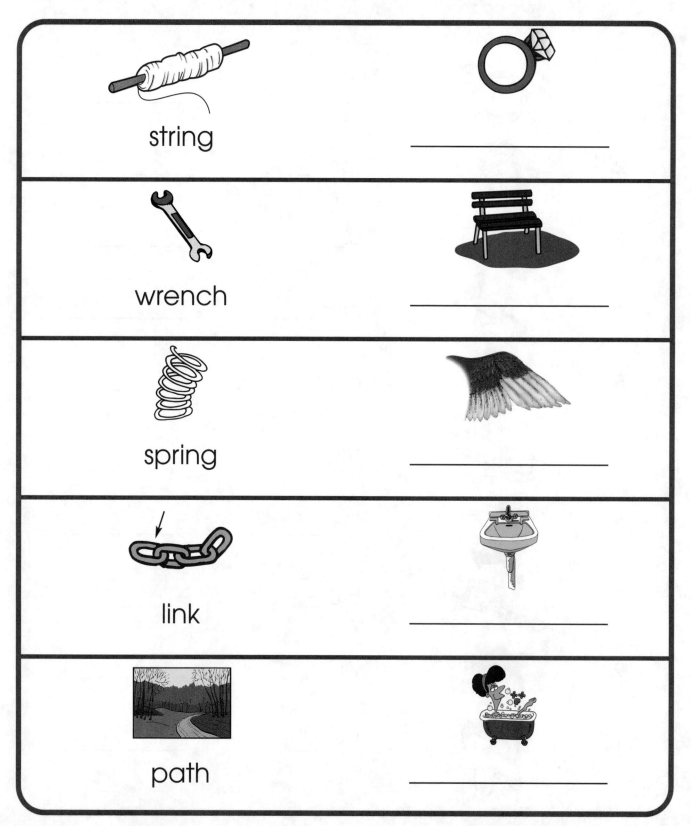

string _____

wrench _____

spring _____

link _____

path _____

Review: Consonant Pairs and Blends

Directions: Write the word from the Word Box that names each picture.

bench	wing	string	chain	watch	path
three	throne	whale	ship	ring	think

Check Up: Consonant Pairs and Blends

Directions: Write the word or words from the Word Box that best completes each sentence.

wing	beach	chunk	bring	bench	cheese
shade	wash	path	ship	splash	shoes

1. The mouse ate a _____ of _____.

2. Mom and Dad sailed on a _____.

3. Can you _____ a snack to the picnic?

4. Patty walked on the _____ in the woods.

5. My sister is sitting on the green _____ in the park.

6. To stay cool, I sit in the _____.

7. The bluebird has a broken _____.

8. At the _____, we like to _____ in the water.

9. You should _____ your dirty _____.

Vowels With R: AR and ER

Directions: Write the word from the Word Box that names each picture.

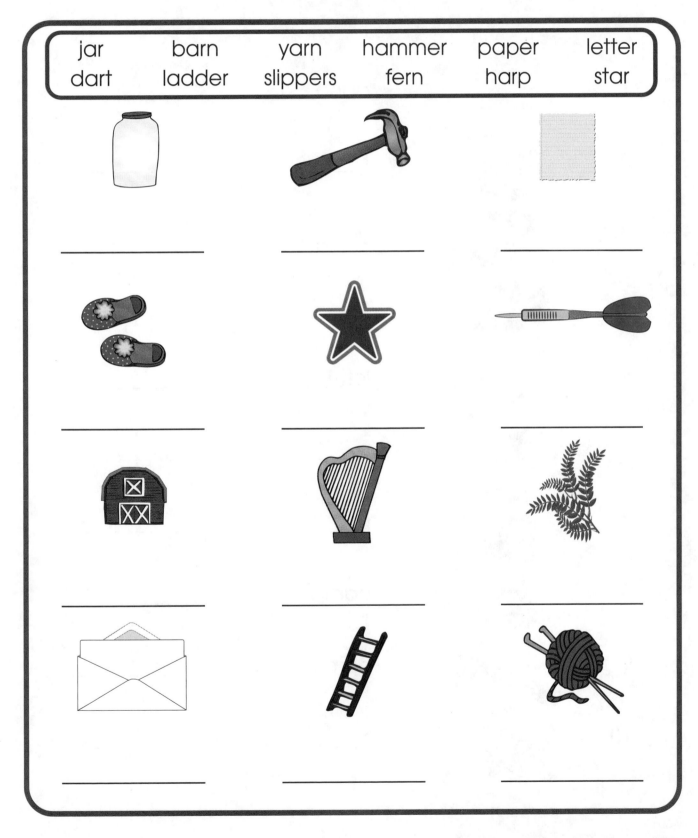

jar	barn	yarn	hammer	paper	letter
dart	ladder	slippers	fern	harp	star

_____   _____   _____

_____   _____   _____

_____   _____   _____

_____   _____   _____

Vowels With R: AR and ER

Directions: Write the missing letters **ar** or **er** for each word. Then, write each word again.

1. danc_____   _____

2. f_____m   _____

3. slipp_____s   _____

4. c_____   _____

5. lett_____   _____

6. y_____n   _____

7. p_____k   _____

8. camp_____   _____

9. hamm_____   _____

10. st_____   _____

Name _____

Vowels With R: IR and OR

Directions: Write the word from the Word Box that names each picture.

dirt	thorn	bird	girl	corn	fort
storm	cork	thirty	fork	shirt	skirt

_____

Name _____

Vowels With R: IR and OR

Directions: Write the missing letters **ir** or **or** for each word. Then, write each word again.

1.   h_____se   _____

2.   sk_____t   _____

3.   f_____k   _____

4.   st_____m   _____

5.   g_____l   _____

6.   c_____n   _____

7.   sh_____t   _____

8.   b_____d   _____

9.   th_____n   _____

10.   c_____d   _____

Name _____

Vowels With R: UR

Directions: Write the word from the Word Box that names each picture.

hurt   fur   turn   burn   curb

_____   _____   _____

_____   _____

Directions: Write two sentences. Use one word from above in each sentence.

1. _____

_____

2. _____

_____

Vowels With R

Directions: Write the word that rhymes with each word below.

horn

_____

car

_____

turn

_____

shirt

_____

thorn

_____

Vowels With R

Directions: Write the word from the Word Box that best completes each sentence.

bird	fur	corn	fern	horn
cart	barn	hurt	bark	

1. The bear's _____ keeps it warm.

2. That _____ is a very pretty plant.

3. Grandpa put the hay in the _____.

4. Grandma ate _____ on the cob for dinner.

5. I _____ my foot playing soccer.

6. Fido will _____ when he wants a bone.

7. The _____ has four wheels.

8. I found a baby _____ in its nest.

9. My sister plays the _____ in the school band.

Name _____

Review: Vowels With R

Directions: Write the word from the Word Box that names each picture.

fork	shirt	hurt	bird	star	burn
letter	turn	fern	horn	car	barn

Check Up: Vowels With R

Directions: Write six sentences. Use one word from the Word Box in each sentence.

| letter | fork | bird | farm | horn | barn |

1. _____

   _____

2. _____

   _____

3. _____

   _____

4. _____

   _____

5. _____

   _____

6. _____

   _____

Name _____

Vowel Pairs: OI and OY

Directions: The vowel pairs **oi** and **oy** can make the sound that you hear in the middle of the words noise and boys. Write the word from the Word Box that names each picture.

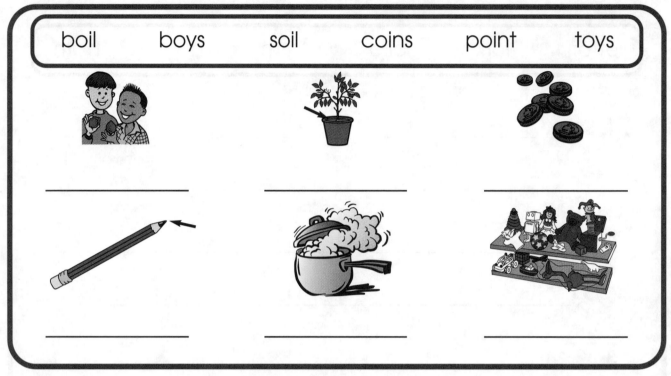

| boil | boys | soil | coins | point | toys |

_____   _____   _____

_____   _____   _____

Directions: Write two sentences. Use one word from above in each sentence.

1. _____

_____

2. _____

_____

Vowel Pairs: OI and OY

Directions: Write the missing letters **oi** or **oy** for each word. Then, write the word again.

1. b_____l _____

2. c_____ns _____

3. b_____s _____

4. s_____l _____

5. _____ster _____

6. _____l _____

7. t_____s _____

8. p_____nt _____

Vowel Pairs: OI and OY

Directions: Write the word from the Word Box that best completes each sentence.

boys	voice	enjoys	noise	point
soil	join	toys	coins	

1. Her loud _____ hurts my ears.

2. I broke the _____ on my pencil.

3. How many _____ do you have in your pocket?

4. We gave the baby two new _____ to play with.

5. Our car is making a funny _____.

6. Those _____ are friends from school.

7. Mark is going to _____ the reading club.

8. We got the _____ ready so we could plant our garden.

9. Mom _____ going to the library.

Vowel Pairs: OU and OW

Directions: The vowel pairs **ou** and **ow** can make the sound you hear in the middle of mouth and clown. Write the word from the Word Box that names each picture.

| shower | pound | plow | crown | house | clown |
| cow | blouse | flower | bounce | frown | gown |

Vowel Pairs: OU and OW

Directions: Write the missing letters **ou** or **ow** for each word. Then, write each word again.

1. cl____d _____

2. m____th _____

3. ____l _____

4. cl____n _____

5. p____nd _____

6. pl____ _____

7. cr____n _____

8. c____ _____

9. fl____er _____

10. h____se _____

Vowel Pairs: OU and OW

Directions: Write the word from the Word Box that best completes each sentence.

cloud	mouse	clown	house	crown
blouse	ground	cow	pound	

1. The queen wears a gold _____.

2. The little _____ likes to nibble on cheese.

3. Dad uses the hammer to _____ nails.

4. The _____ did funny tricks.

5. Mom has a pretty blue _____ and skirt.

6. The _____ likes to munch on grass.

7. There is a puffy white _____ in the sky.

8. I dropped my watch on the _____.

9. My _____ is not far from school.

Name _____

Review: Vowel Pairs

Directions: Write the word that rhymes with each word below.

gown _____

blouse _____

boys _____

soil _____

plow _____

Name _____

Check Up: Vowel Pairs

Directions: Write a word that names each picture. Each word should have the **oi**, **oy**, **ou**, or **ow** vowel pair.

Name _____

Letters and Their Sounds

bat   gate   pail

car   sauce   fawn

tray   cup   mice

chain   chicks   web

seal   thread   tree

Name _____

Letters and Their Sounds

lett**er**

sc**rew**

game

ca**g**e

hit

f**i**ve

sk**ir**t

knee

wi**ng**

f**o**x

s**oa**p

r**o**se

oil

sp**oo**n

h**oo**k

Name _____

Letters and Their Sounds

corn

h**ou**se

cr**ow**

owl

b**oy**s

ship

think

throat

r**u**g

m**u**le

b**ur**n

whale

wrench

sk**y**

pupp**y**

Name _____

Practice Page

Name _____

Practice Page

Name _____

Practice Page

Name _____

Practice Page

Answer Key

Review: Beginning and Ending Sounds

Directions: Say the name of each picture. Write the missing letter or letters to complete each word.

ta_g_	_v_ an
_b_ u _s_	_m_ op
si _x_	_s_ u _n_
_w_ eb	_h_ _a_ _t_ _c_ _a_ _p_

6

Name

Review: Beginning and Ending Sounds

Directions: Say the name of each picture. Write the missing letter or letters to complete each word.

_c_ an	_m_ a _p_
do _g_	_p_ i _g_
_t_ op	be _d_
_f_ a _n_	_h_ a _m_

7

Name

Short a

Directions: Connect all the pictures whose names have the short **a** sound from the cat to the bag.

8

Name

Short a

Directions: Write the word from the Word Box that names each picture.

van	cab	hat	apple	map	pan
add	ham	ant	can	hand	ax

cab	ant	van
apple	map	pan
hand	4+1=5 add	can
ham	hat	ax

9

Answer Key

Answer Key

Name _____

Short a

Directions: Write the word from the Word Box that best completes each sentence.

pan hand hat has ant as ham apple am

1. An __ant__ is very tiny.

2. Can you __hand__ Dad the bag?

3. I wear a __hat__ .

4. I __am__ glad.

5. He is __as__ tall as a yardstick.

6. Mom will fry fish in a __pan__ .

7. We had __ham__ for lunch.

8. She __has__ a new hat.

9. The __apple__ is red.

10

Name _____

Short e

Directions: Write the word from the Word Box that names each picture.

desk	bed	net	tent	web	leg
nest	hen	egg	jet	belt	dress

bed egg net

leg hen jet

belt tent desk

web dress nest

11

Name _____

Short e

Directions: Write a word that rhymes with each word below.

1. nest — Answers will vary. Examples: __vest__

2. net — __bet__

3. jet — __wet__

4. sled — __bed__

__pen__

Directions: Draw a picture of something whose name has the short e sound. Then, write the word that names the picture.

Answers will vary

_____

12

Name _____

Short e

Directions: Write the word from the Word Box that best completes each sentence.

beg	smell	net	wet	nest

1. Dad had the frog in a __net__ .

2. The bird sleeps in its __nest__ .

3. Can you __smell__ the flower?

4. The shirt is __wet__ .

5. My dog likes to __beg__ .

Directions: Write two short e words of your own. Then, use each word in a sentence.

1. _____ 2. _____

1. _____

Answers will vary

2. _____

13

Spectrum Phonics Grade 2

Answer Key

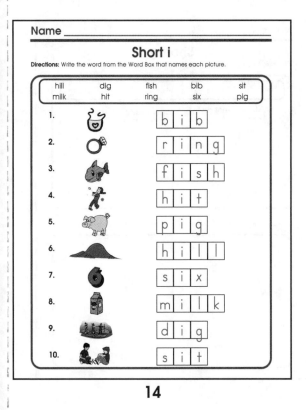

Name _____

Short i

Directions: Write the word from the Word Box that names each picture.

hill	dig	fish	bib	sit
milk	hit	ring	six	pig

1. b i b
2. r i n g
3. f i s h
4. h i t
5. p i g
6. h i l l
7. s i x
8. m i l k
9. d i g
10. s i t

14

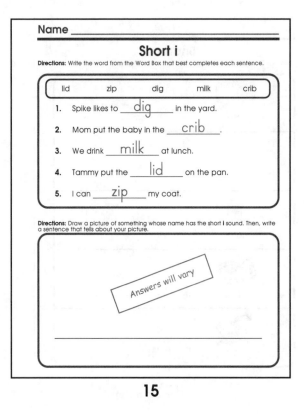

Name _____

Short i

Directions: Write the word from the Word Box that best completes each sentence.

lid	zip	dig	milk	crib

1. Spike likes to __dig__ in the yard.
2. Mom put the baby in the __crib__ .
3. We drink __milk__ at lunch.
4. Tammy put the __lid__ on the pan.
5. I can __zip__ my coat.

Directions: Draw a picture of something whose name has the short i sound. Then, write a sentence that tells about your picture.

Answers will vary

_____

15

Name _____

Short i

Directions: Draw a picture of something that rhymes with each word below. Then, write the rhyming word.

pig _____

bib _____

grill   Answers will vary

fish _____

hit _____

16

Name _____

Short o

Directions: Write the word from the Word Box that names each picture.

dots	cot	lock	cob	box	doll
rod	top	pot	hop	fox	mop

cot   rod   doll

mop   fox   lock

dots   box   pot

hop   top   cob

17

Answer Key

Answer Key

Name _____

Short o

Directions: Draw a picture of something that rhymes with each word below. Then, write the rhyming word.

box _____

mop _____

lock _____ *Answers will vary*

spot _____

frog _____

18

Name _____

Short o

Directions: Write the word from the Word Box that best completes each sentence.

| hop | top | cot | hot | chop |

1. Molly sleeps on the ___cot___ .
2. Dad can ___chop___ with the ax.
3. The pot is very ___hot___ .
4. The bunny likes to ___hop___ .
5. Can you spin a ___top___ ?

Directions: Draw a picture of something whose name has the short **o** sound. Then, write a sentence that tells about your picture.

Answers will vary

_____

19

Name _____

Short u

Directions: Write the word from the Word Box that names each picture.

| run | cub | pup | tub | nut | sun |
| bus | mug | hug | bug | bun | rug |

tub   mug   rug

sun   cub   pup

hug   bun   nut

run   bug   bus

20

Name _____

Short u

Directions: Draw a picture of something that rhymes with each word below. Then, write the rhyming word.

bun _____

jump _____

hug _____ *Answers will vary*

cub _____

pup _____

21

Answer Key

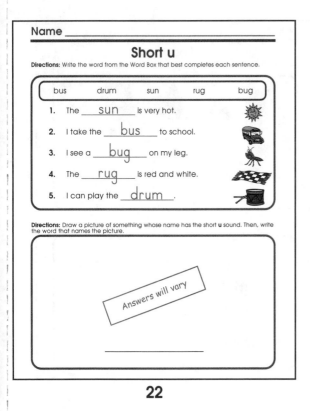

Name _____

Short u

Directions: Write the word from the Word Box that best completes each sentence.

bus	drum	sun	rug	bug

1. The __sun__ is very hot.
2. I take the __bus__ to school.
3. I see a __bug__ on my leg.
4. The __rug__ is red and white.
5. I can play the __drum__ .

Directions: Draw a picture of something whose name has the short **u** sound. Then, write the word that names the picture.

Answers will vary

_____

22

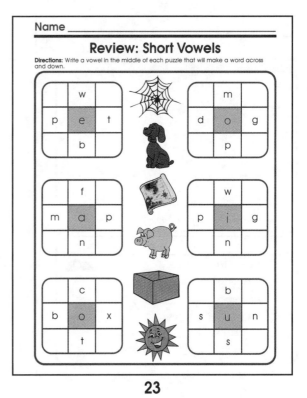

Name _____

Review: Short Vowels

Directions: Write a vowel in the middle of each puzzle that will make a word across and down.

p **e** t, w, b

m **a** p, f, n

b **o** x, c, t

d **o** g, m, p

p **i** g, w, n

s **u** n, b, s

23

Name _____

Check Up: Short Vowels

Directions: Write the word from the Word Box that names each picture.

fox	jump	tag	bed	cup	six	top	map

fox   map
cup   bed
six   top
tag   jump

Directions: Write a word that has each short vowel sound listed below. Use different words than those above.

1. a _____   4. o _____
2. e _____   5. u _____
3. i _____

Answers will vary

24

Name _____

Long a

Directions: Circle each picture that has the long **a** sound.

Directions: Fill in the missing letters **a** and **e** for each word. Then, write each word again.

1. r **a** k **e**   rake
2. c **a** p **e**   cape
3. s **a** f **e**   safe
4. v **a** s **e**   vase
5. c **a** n **e**   cane

25

Spectrum Phonics Grade 2

133

Answer Key

Answer Key

Name _____

Long a

Directions: Draw a picture of something that has the long **a** sound. Then, write a sentence that tells about your picture.

> Answers will vary

_____

Directions: Write the word from the Word Box that best completes each sentence.

| ape | lake | cane | vase | bake | game |

1. We swim in the __lake__.
2. Mom put flowers in the __vase__.
3. Sam plays a __game__.
4. I will __bake__ a cake.
5. Grandpa needs a __cane__ to walk.
6. We saw an __ape__ at the zoo.

26

Name _____

Long i

Directions: Draw a line to match each picture with its name.

bite   slide   line   hive   pine

Directions: Write the missing letters **i** and **e** for each word. Then, write each word again.

1. f i v e   five
2. v i n e   vine
3. k i t e   kite
4. b i k e   bike

27

Name _____

Long i

Directions: Draw a picture of something that has the long **i** sound. Then, write the word that names the picture.

> Answers will vary

_____

Directions: Write the word from the Word Box that best completes each sentence.

| bite | dive | kite | ride | bike | pine |

1. My __kite__ is up in the tree.
2. I ride my __bike__ to school.
3. I like the smell of __pine__ trees.
4. Can you __ride__ a horse?
5. Take a __bite__ of the pizza.
6. Dave will __dive__ into the pool.

28

Name _____

Long o

Directions: Write the word from the Word Box that names each picture.

| stove | cone | pole | rope | bone | nose |

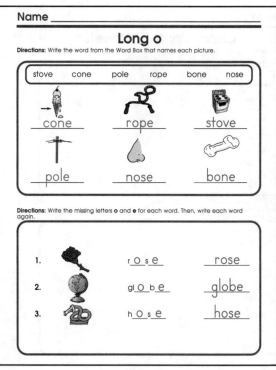

cone   rope   stove

pole   nose   bone

Directions: Write the missing letters **o** and **e** for each word. Then, write each word again.

1. r o s e   rose
2. gl o b e   globe
3. h o s e   hose

29

Spectrum Phonics Grade 2

134

Answer Key

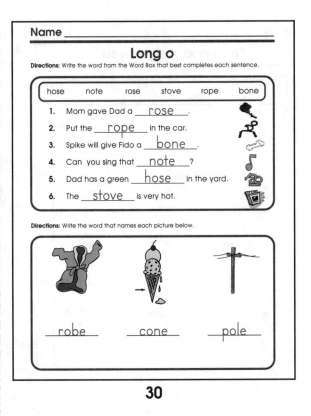

Name _____

Long o

Directions: Write the word from the Word Box that best completes each sentence.

hose	note	rose	stove	rope	bone

1. Mom gave Dad a __rose__ .
2. Put the __rope__ in the car.
3. Spike will give Fido a __bone__ .
4. Can you sing that __note__ ?
5. Dad has a green __hose__ in the yard.
6. The __stove__ is very hot.

Directions: Write the word that names each picture below.

__robe__   __cone__   __pole__

30

Name _____

Long u

Directions: Write the missing letters **u** and **e** for each word. Then, write each word again.

1. t u_ n e __tune__
2. m u l e __mule__
3. d u_ n e __dune__
4. c u t e __cute__
5. c u b e __cube__

Directions: Write a word that rhymes with each word below.

Answers will vary

1. tube   Examples: __cube__
2. prune   __tune__
3. flute   __cute__

31

Name _____

Long u

Directions: Circle the word that names the picture. Then, write the word on the line.

cub / (cube) / cup	rug / mule / (ruler)	mug / (mule) / tune
__cube__	__ruler__	__mule__
cute / (flute) / fun	(tune) / nut / tube	den / (dune) / tune
__flute__	__tune__	__dune__
dune / tune / (prune)	tub / tuba / (tube)	(cute) / cut / cube
__prune__	__tube__	__cute__

32

Name _____

Review: Long Vowels

Directions: Write the missing vowels to complete each word.

1. r a_ k e __rake__
2. r o_ b e __robe__
3. t a_ p e __tape__
4. t u_ b e __tube__
5. k i_ t e __kite__

Directions: Write a word that rhymes with each word below.

Answers will vary. Examples:

1. vine __pine__   5. wave __save__
2. gate __late__   6. like __bike__
3. hose __nose__   7. tune __dune__
4. cube __tube__   8. game __tame__

33

Answer Key

Name _____

Check Up: Long Vowels

Directions: Write the word from the Word Box that names each picture.

cape	safe	bike	vase	mule	bone
tube	prune	hose	cone	cube	nine

bike   hose   vase

cape   nine   cube

prune   cone   mule

bone   hide   safe

34

Name _____

Short and Long Vowels

Directions: Write the word from the Word Box that names each picture.

duck	pan	rod	skates	lips	tape
cub	dress	slide	cone	vine	flute

cub   cone   duck

vine   tape   rod

pan   flute   dress

skate   lips   slide

35

Name _____

Short and Long Vowels

Directions: Write each picture name in the correct column.

Short Vowel Words	Long Vowel Words
six	hive
desk	cone
fox	flute
sun	safe
bat	ape
tub	tube

36

Name _____

Short and Long Vowels

Directions: Write the missing vowel or vowels for each word.

1. b <u>u</u> g
2. b <u>a</u> k <u>e</u>
3. r <u>o</u> p <u>e</u>
4. b <u>e</u> d
5. n <u>o</u> s <u>e</u>
6. t <u>o</u> p
7. m <u>a</u> p
8. m <u>u</u> l <u>e</u>
9. b <u>i</u> b
10. p <u>i</u> n <u>e</u>

37

Answer Key

Name _____

Short and Long Vowels

Directions: Draw a picture of something whose name has the vowel sound written in each box. Then, write the word that names each picture.

Long u	Short a	Short e
_____	_____	_____

Long i	Long o	Short i
	Answers will vary	
_____	_____	_____

Short u	Long a	Short o
_____	_____	_____

38

Name _____

Check Up: Short and Long Vowels

Directions: Circle the word that best completes each sentence. Then, write the word in the blank.

1. Lisa put the hat in the __box__ .
   bone   (box)   robe

2. A __hog__ is a very large animal.
   hag   hose   (hog)

3. The mother bear takes care of her __cub__ .
   cube   cup   (cub)

4. Let's play a __game__ .
   gum   gate   (game)

5. I will play a __tune__ on the flute.
   tub   tube   (tune)

6. Put the __rope__ on the boat.
   robe   (rope)   nine

7. I like to go down the __slide__ .
   five   fish   (slide)

8. He will wash the dog in the __tub__ .
   (tub)   tube   tag

39

Name _____

Hard and Soft c

Directions: The letter **c** can have the hard sound of **k**. It can also have the soft sound of **s**. Draw a line to match each word with its picture.

Hard **c** = calf   Soft **c** = cent

cot   ice   city   coat

Directions: Write each picture name from above in the correct column.

Hard c Words	Soft c Words
cot	city
calf	ice

40

Name _____

Hard and Soft c

Directions: Write the word from the Word Box that names each picture.

pencil	city	fence	cow	ice	mice
car	cup	cent	cab	face	cap

car   cow   cent

ice   mice   cab

cap   pencil   cup

fence   face   city

41

Answer Key

Name _____

Hard and Soft g

Directions: The letter **g** can have a hard sound and a soft sound. Draw a line to match each word with its picture.

Hard **g** = gas   Soft **g** = bridge

cage   stage   garden   game

Directions: Write each picture name from above in the correct column.

Hard g Words	Soft g Words
garden	cage
game	stage

42

Name _____

Hard and Soft g

Directions: Write the word from the Word Box that names each picture.

wig	edge	judge	goat	gate	cage
stage	globe	dog	page	bridge	pig

edge   goat   dog

page   wig   judge

cage   globe   pig

gate   bridge   stage

43

Name _____

Review: Hard and Soft c and g

Directions: Write the missing letter **c** or **g** for each word. Then, circle the word *hard* or *soft* to tell how the letter sounds.

1. _g_ as — (hard) soft
2. sta _g_ e — hard (soft)
3. _C_ age — (hard) soft
4. fa _C_ e — hard (soft)
5. i _C_ e — hard (soft)
6. brid _g_ e — hard (soft)
7. _C_ alf — (hard) soft
8. _g_ arden — (hard) soft
9. jud _g_ e — hard (soft)
10. mi _C_ e — hard (soft)

44

Name _____

Check Up: Hard and Soft c and g

Directions: Circle the word that best completes each sentence. Then, write the word in the blank.

1. Mom has on a __lace__ dress.
   leg   (lace)   place
2. We will drive across the __bridge__.
   judge   fence   (bridge)
3. We saw a __goat__ at the farm.
   (goat)   gas   edge
4. Dad goes to work in the __city__.
   ice   fence   (city)
5. Emily wears a __coat__ when it is cold.
   cow   cab   (coat)
6. What do you plant in your __garden__?
   cup   cage   (garden)
7. Mom does not like __mice__.
   edge   (mice)   pencil
8. The __judge__ is a kind man.
   (judge)   page   cent

45

Spectrum Phonics Grade 2

Answer Key

Answer Key

Name _____

Consonant Blends With S

Directions: Write the consonant blend that shows the beginning sound of each picture name.

| sn | sk | st | sm | sl | sw |

__sn__ake   __st__ore   __sk__ates

__sl__ide   __st__eps   __sm__oke

__sw__ing   __sm__ile   __sn__ail

__sk__unk   __st__age   __sl__eep

46

Name _____

Consonant Blends With S

Directions: Write the word from the Word Box that names each picture.

| square | snap | spoon | sled | store | scare |

__spoon__   __scare__   __sled__

__snap__   __square__   __store__

Directions: Write two sentences. Use one word from above in each sentence.

1. _____

2. _____

Sentences will vary

47

Name _____

Consonant Blends With L

Directions: Write the consonant blend that shows the beginning sound of each picture name.

| pl | cl | fl | gl | bl |

__cl__am   __fl__ower   __bl__ock

__fl__ag   __gl__obe   __pl__ate

__pl__ug   __cl__ap   __cl__ub

__cl__own   __fl__ute   __pl__ane

48

Name _____

Consonant Blends With L

Directions: Write the word from the Word Box that names each picture.

| blow | clip | flame | glass | fly | flute |

__clip__   __flame__   __fly__

__flute__   __blow__   __glass__

Directions: Write two sentences. Use one word from above in each sentence.

1. _____

2. _____

Sentences will vary

49

Answer Key

Name _____

Consonant Blends With R

Directions: Write the consonant blend that shows the beginning sound of each picture name.

dr	br	cr	fr	tr	pr

__br__ide   __fr__og   __cr__ow

__br__idge   __cr__ab   __dr__ess

__dr__um   __tr__ap   __pr__ize

__br__oom   __fr__ame   __fr__uit

50

Name _____

Consonant Blends With R

Directions: Write the word from the Word Box that names each picture.

crayon	tray	prince	dress	crown	tree

__tray__   __prince__   __crayon__

__tree__   __dress__   __crown__

Directions: Write two sentences. Use one word from above in each sentence.

1. _____

2. _____

Sentences will vary

51

Name _____

Review: Consonant Blends

Directions: Write the word from the Word Box that names each picture.

bridge	stage	snake	grass	tree	crab
crown	sled	globe	flag	plug	bride

__crown__   __globe__   __tree__

__bride__   __sled__   __snake__

__grass__   __plug__   __stage__

__bridge__   __flag__   __crab__

52

Name _____

Final Consonant Blends

Directions: Write the final consonant blend for each word. Then, write each word again.

1. ca__st__   __cast__
2. de__sk__   __desk__
3. roa__st__   __roast__
4. toa__st__   __toast__
5. ma__sk__   __mask__

Directions: Write the word that rhymes with each word below.

1. mist   __list__
2. vest   __nest__
3. roast   __toast__

53

Answer Key

Name _____

Final Consonant Blends

Directions: Circle the consonant blend that you hear at the end of each picture name.

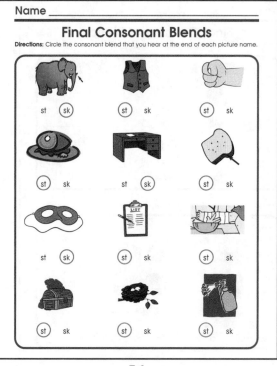

54

Name _____

Review: Final Consonant Blends

Directions: Write the word from the Word Box that names each picture.

| mask | list | vest | desk | fist | mist |
| chest | tusk | roast | nest | crust | toast |

chest   vest   desk

mist   crust   mask

tusk   roast   fist

list   nest   toast

55

Name _____

Final Consonant Blends

Directions: Write the final consonant blend of each word. Then, write each word again.

1. sta__mp__   __stamp__
2. pai __nt__   __paint__
3. sku __nk__   __skunk__
4. pla __nt__   __plant__
5. ce __nt__   __cent__

Directions: Write a word that rhymes with each word below.

1. band   __hand__
2. stump   __pump__
3. sink   __link__

56

Name _____

Final Consonant Blends

Directions: Circle the word that names each picture.

(pond) / point / paint   bank / (crank) / cent

stand / cent / (tent)   pump / (paint) / plant

(lamp) / pump / stump   wink / sink / (wind)

band / (bank) / pond   (ant) / stand / and

stump / (stamp) / stand   stump / pond / (pump)

57

Answer Key

Name _____

Review: Final Consonant Blends

Directions: Write the word from the Word Box that names each picture.

cast	cent	mask	hand	plant	lamp
skunk	sink	pond	desk	bank	stamp

mask   skunk   hand

bank   stamp   cent

sink   plant   pond

desk   cast   lamp

58

Name _____

Final Consonant Blends

Directions: Write the final consonant blend to complete each word. Then, write each word again.

1. ra __ft__   raft
2. qui __lt__   quilt
3. wo __lf__   wolf
4. wi __lt__   wilt
5. go __lf__   golf

Directions: Write the word that rhymes with each word below.

1. shelf   elf
2. lift   gift
3. melt   belt

59

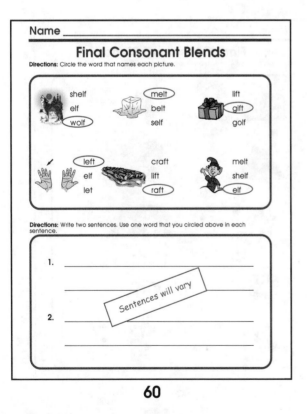

Name _____

Final Consonant Blends

Directions: Circle the word that names each picture.

shelf   (melt)   lift
elf   belt   (gift)
(wolf)   self   golf

(left)   craft   melt
elf   lift   shelf
let   (raft)   (elf)

Directions: Write two sentences. Use one word that you circled above in each sentence.

1. _____

Sentences will vary

2. _____

60

Name _____

Review: Final Consonant Blends

Directions: Write the word from the Word Box that names each picture.

wilt	belt	raft	quilt	lift	wolf	shelf	left

belt   lift   shelf   quilt

raft   wolf   wilt   left

Directions: Look at the picture and write the word that best completes each sentence.

1. The __elf__ is very small.
2. Mom gave Dad a __gift__.
3. Do you play __golf__?
4. Put the books on the __shelf__.
5. The ice will __melt__ in the sun.

61

Answer Key

Answer Key

Name _____

Three-Letter Consonant Blends

Directions: Write a three-letter consonant blend to complete each word. Then, write each word again.

1. <u>str</u> eet   <u>street</u>
2. <u>scr</u> ew   <u>screw</u>
3. <u>spl</u> it   <u>split</u>
4. <u>scr</u> eam   <u>scream</u>
5. <u>str</u> eam   <u>stream</u>
6. <u>scr</u> ub   <u>scrub</u>
7. <u>spl</u> ash   <u>splash</u>
8. <u>spr</u> ing   <u>spring</u>
9. <u>str</u> ap   <u>strap</u>
10. <u>str</u> ong   <u>strong</u>

62

Name _____

Three-Letter Consonant Blends

Directions: Draw a picture to go with each word below. Then, write a sentence that tells about each picture. Make sure to use the word in the sentence.

scream	street
splash	scrub

Answers will vary

63

Name _____

Three-Letter Consonant Blends

Directions: Write the word from the Word Box that best completes each sentence.

stripes	scrape	street	sprain	scrub
spray	scrap	splash	stream	

1. There are many houses on my <u>street</u> .
2. Dad will <u>spray</u> the garden with the hose.
3. Steve makes a big <u>splash</u> when he jumps in the pool.
4. Write your name on this <u>scrap</u> of paper.
5. Grandpa and I fish in the <u>stream</u> .
6. I do not like to <u>scrub</u> the floor.
7. Oliver has a <u>scrape</u> on his knee.
8. My new kitten has black and gray <u>stripes</u> .
9. Mom got a bad <u>sprain</u> when she fell.

64

Name _____

Review: 3-Letter Consonant Blends

Directions: Write the word from the Word Box that names each picture.

scream	stripes	strap	street	strong	scrub
screw	spring	string	split	splash	stream

<u>strap</u>   <u>stripes</u>   <u>splash</u>

<u>string</u>   <u>scream</u>   <u>stream</u>

<u>screw</u>   <u>street</u>   <u>split</u>

<u>scrub</u>   <u>strong</u>   <u>spring</u>

65

Answer Key

Check Up: Consonant Blends

Directions: Write a consonant blend to complete each word.

1. <u>spr</u>ing
2. <u>fl</u>ag
3. <u>tr</u>ay
4. <u>spl</u>it
5. de<u>sk</u>
6. <u>cl</u>own
7. sku<u>nk</u>
8. ne<u>st</u>
9. <u>sp</u>oon
10. <u>sn</u>ake
11. <u>br</u>idge
12. <u>fr</u>og

66

Name _____

Silent Consonants

Directions: Write **kn** or **wr** to show the letters that make the beginning sound of each picture name.

The letters **kn** make the sound of **n**.
The letters **wr** make the sound of **r**.

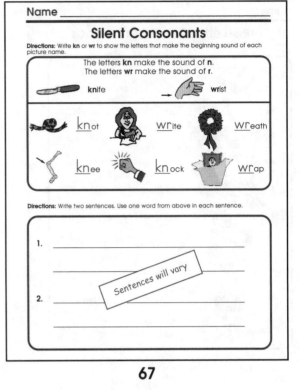

knife   wrist

<u>kn</u>ot   <u>wr</u>ite   <u>wr</u>eath

<u>kn</u>ee   <u>kn</u>ock   <u>wr</u>ap

Directions: Write two sentences. Use one word from above in each sentence.

1. _____

2. _____

Sentences will vary

67

Name _____

Silent Consonants

Directions: Write the word from the Word Box that names each picture.

| wrench | knock | wrist | kneel | write | knit |

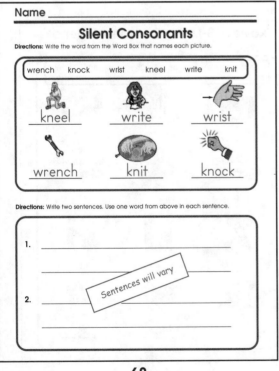

kneel   write   wrist

wrench   knit   knock

Directions: Write two sentences. Use one word from above in each sentence.

1. _____

2. _____

Sentences will vary

68

Name _____

Silent Consonants

Directions: Write the word from the Word Box that best completes each sentence.

| knot | write | wrap | knife | |
| know | knock | knee | knit | wrong |

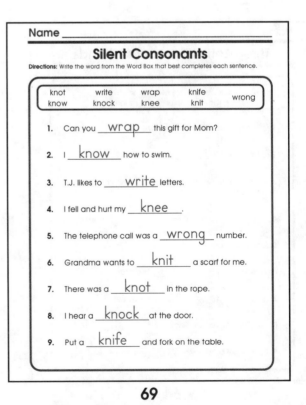

1. Can you <u>wrap</u> this gift for Mom?

2. I <u>know</u> how to swim.

3. T.J. likes to <u>write</u> letters.

4. I fell and hurt my <u>knee</u>.

5. The telephone call was a <u>wrong</u> number.

6. Grandma wants to <u>knit</u> a scarf for me.

7. There was a <u>knot</u> in the rope.

8. I hear a <u>knock</u> at the door.

9. Put a <u>knife</u> and fork on the table.

69

Answer Key

Answer Key

Name _____

Silent Consonants

Directions: Write the word from the Word Box that names each picture.

The letters **ck** make the sound of **k**.

du**ck**

rock	dock	pocket	brick	
jacket	clock	rocket	tack	truck

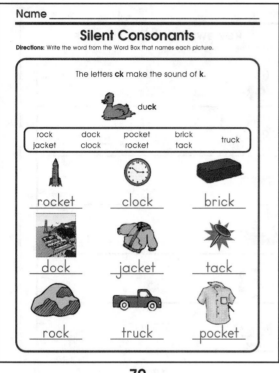

rocket   clock   brick

dock   jacket   tack

rock   truck   pocket

70

Name _____

Silent Consonants

Directions: Draw a picture to go with each word below. Then, write a sentence that tells about each picture. Make sure to use the word in the sentence.

pocket	rocket
truck	rock

Answers will vary

71

Name _____

Silent Consonants

Directions: Write the word from the Word Box that best completes each sentence.

pack	duck	snack	chicks	
clock	tricks	lock	black	dock

1. Did you hear that __duck__ quack?

2. My __clock__ shows the wrong time.

3. Grandma has baby __chicks__ at the farm.

4. Dad gave me a __lock__ for my bike.

5. My dog has __black__ and white fur.

6. Mom steered the boat to the __dock__.

7. Dave put his books in his __pack__.

8. Matt likes to play __tricks__ on his friends.

9. I am hungry for a __snack__.

72

Name _____

Silent Consonants

Directions: Write the word from the Word Box that names each picture.

When **g** and **h** are together in a word, they are often silent.

8 eig**h**t

| eighty | light | knight | high | bright | night |

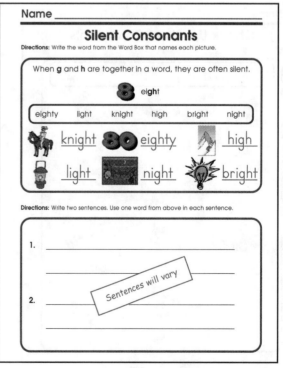

knight   eighty   high

light   night   bright

Directions: Write two sentences. Use one word from above in each sentence.

1. _____

2. _____

Sentences will vary

73

Answer Key

Answer Key

Silent Consonants

Name _____

Silent Consonants

Directions: Write the word from the Word Box that best completes each sentence.

might	right	fight	night	
tight	eighty	light	high	sight

1. Grandpa is almost __eighty__ years old.

2. We __might__ not have school tomorrow.

3. My red jacket is too __tight__.

4. Mom was __right__ about the storm.

5. The snowy trees are a pretty __sight__.

6. The __light__ is very bright.

7. It rained all __night__ long.

8. I can't reach that __high__ shelf.

9. Dad doesn't like it when we __fight__.

74

Name _____

Review: Silent Consonants

Directions: Write a sentence that tells about each picture.

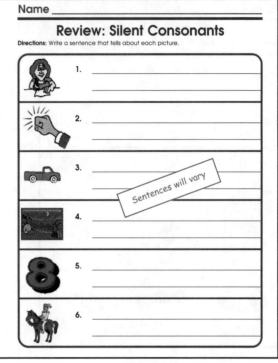

1. _____

2. _____

3. _____

Sentences will vary

4. _____

5. _____

6. _____

75

Name _____

Check Up: Silent Consonants

Directions: Write the word from the Word Box that names each picture.

chicks	rock	lock	knit	knight	knock
wrist	write	pocket	wrap	knot	light

knight   rock   write

pocket   chicks   knot

knit   light   knock

wrist   wrap   lock

76

Name _____

Vowel Pairs: AI and AY

Directions: The vowel pairs **ai** and **ay** can make the long **a** sound. Write the word that rhymes with each word below.

train   rain

tail   pail

tray   hay

clay   pay

snail   mail

77

Answer Key

Name _____

Vowel Pairs: AI and AY

Directions: Write the word from the Word Box that names each picture.

clay	pail	tail	train	paint	mail
rain	stain	chain	pay	sail	tray

pail   stain   tray

rain   tail   sail

paint   chain   train

clay   pay   mail

78

Name _____

Vowel Pairs: AI and AY

Directions: Write the word from the Word Box that best completes each sentence.

paint	tray	mail	snail	
rain	tail	clay	train	hay

1. The __snail__ is in its shell.

2. Dad brought us cookies on a __tray__.

3. The cows eat __hay__.

4. Kelly made a bowl from __clay__.

5. We don't like to play outside in the __rain__.

6. Fluffy wags his __tail__ when he is happy.

7. What color __paint__ should we use?

8. Grandma took the __train__ when she came to see us.

9. I bring in the __mail__ every day.

79

Name _____

Vowel Pairs: EE and EA

Directions: The vowel pairs **ee** and **ea** can make the long **e** sound. Write the word from the Word Box that names each picture.

beads	tree	seal	bee	feet	seat

bee   seal   feet

tree   beads   seat

Directions: Write two sentences. Use one word from above in each sentence.

1. _____

2. _____

Sentences will vary

80

Name _____

Vowel Pairs: EE and EA

Directions: Draw a picture to go with each word below. Then, write a sentence that tells about each picture. Make sure to use the word in the sentence.

leaf	beach
feet	sleep

Answers will vary

81

Answer Key

Answer Key

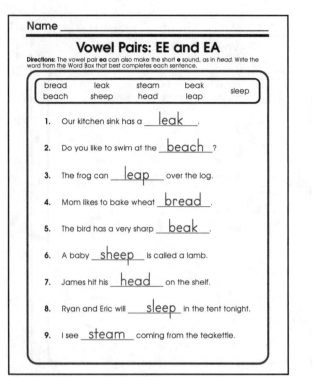

Name _____

Vowel Pairs: EE and EA

Directions: The vowel pair **ea** can also make the short **e** sound, as in *head*. Write the word from the Word Box that best completes each sentence.

| bread | leak | steam | beak | sleep |
| beach | sheep | head | leap | |

1. Our kitchen sink has a __leak__ .

2. Do you like to swim at the __beach__ ?

3. The frog can __leap__ over the log.

4. Mom likes to bake wheat __bread__ .

5. The bird has a very sharp __beak__ .

6. A baby __sheep__ is called a lamb.

7. James hit his __head__ on the shelf.

8. Ryan and Eric will __sleep__ in the tent tonight.

9. I see __steam__ coming from the teakettle.

82

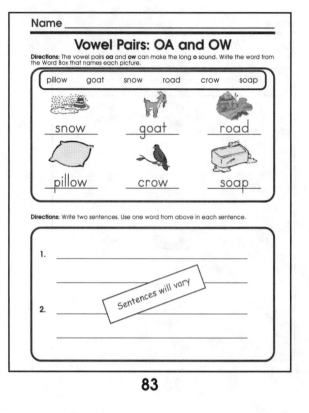

Name _____

Vowel Pairs: OA and OW

Directions: The vowel pairs **oa** and **ow** can make the long **o** sound. Write the word from the Word Box that names each picture.

| pillow | goat | snow | road | crow | soap |

__snow__   __goat__   __road__

__pillow__   __crow__   __soap__

Directions: Write two sentences. Use one word from above in each sentence.

1. _____

2. _____

Sentences will vary

83

Name _____

Vowel Pairs: OA and OW

Directions: Draw a picture to go with each word below. Then, write a sentence that tells about each picture. Make sure to use the word in the sentence.

| **coat** | **window** |
| **bowl** | **toad** |

Answers will vary

84

Name _____

Vowel Pairs: OA and OW

Directions: Write the word from the Word Box that best completes each sentence.

| toad | row | grown | goat | pillow |
| bowl | throw | toast | coat | |

1. A baby __goat__ is called a kid.

2. Can you __throw__ the ball to Amy?

3. I left my new wool __coat__ at school.

4. Mom gave me a soft __pillow__ .

5. That __toad__ has bumpy skin.

6. Let's make a __bowl__ of popcorn.

7. The baby has __grown__ a lot in three months.

8. Dad made eggs and __toast__ for breakfast.

9. We can __row__ the boat into the middle of the lake.

85

Answer Key

Name

Review: Vowel Pairs

Directions: Write the missing vowel pair for each word. Then, write each word again.

1. b_ea_k — beak
2. h_ay_ — hay
3. s_oa_p — soap
4. br_ea_d — bread
5. sl_ee_p — sleep
6. b_ow_l — bowl
7. s_ea_l — seal
8. sn_ai_l — snail
9. l_ea_f — leaf
10. cr_ow_ — crow

86

Name

Vowel Pair: OO

Directions: The vowel pair **oo** can make a short sound, as in *hook*, and a long sound, as in *moon*. Write the word that rhymes with each word below.

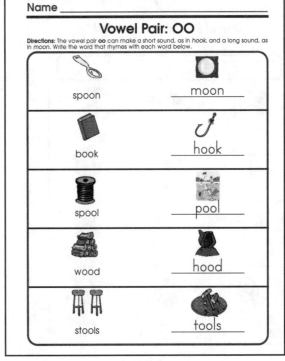

spoon	moon
book	hook
spool	pool
wood	hood
stools	tools

87

Name

Vowel Pair: OO

Directions: Write the word from the Word Box that names each picture.

| spoon | boot | moose | hoop | moon | pool |
| woods | tooth | hood | hoof | broom | book |

boot   tooth   broom

hoop   moose   hoof

woods   book   spoon

moon   hood   pool

88

Name

Vowel Pairs: AU and AW

Directions: The vowel pairs **au** and **aw** can make the sound that you hear in the middle of the words *cause* and *lawn*. In each row, write the two words that rhyme with the first word in the row.

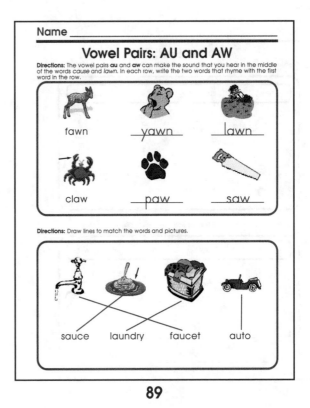

fawn   yawn   lawn

claw   paw   saw

Directions: Draw lines to match the words and pictures.

sauce   laundry   faucet   auto

89

Answer Key

Name _____

Vowel Pairs: AU and AW
Directions: Write the word from the Word Box that names each picture.

straw	saw	crawl	fawn	auto	claw
paw	sauce	yawn	faucet	laundry	lawn

crawl   auto   saw

faucet   straw   laundry

fawn   sauce   lawn

yawn   paw   claw

90

Name _____

Vowel Pairs: AU and AW
Directions: Write the word from the Word Box that best completes each sentence.

fawn	caught	straw	auto	lawn
faucet	crawl	shawl	saw	

1. Dad put a new __faucet__ on the sink.

2. A baby deer is called a __fawn__.

3. Mom cut the wood with a __saw__.

4. My baby brother is just learning to __crawl__.

5. The fish got __caught__ in the net.

6. Our family bought a new car at the __auto__ show.

7. The __lawn__ is nice and green in the spring.

8. Grandma wears a __shawl__ to keep warm.

9. Ryan sips his milk through a __straw__.

91

Name _____

Vowel Pair: EW
Directions: The vowel pair **ew** can make the long **u** sound. Write the word from the Word Box that names each picture.

news	stew	jewelry	screw

1. jewelry   3. screw

2. news   4. stew

Directions: Write two sentences. Use one word from the Word Box in each sentence.

flew	new	few	grew

1. _____

2. _____

Sentences will vary

92

Name _____

Vowel Pair: EW
Directions: Write the word from the Word Box that best completes each sentence.

chew	grew	dew	jewelry	stew
drew	few	flew	news	

1. Last year, we __grew__ beans in our garden.

2. We went to the beach a __few__ times this summer.

3. There is __dew__ on the lawn in the morning.

4. Have you heard the good __news__ ?

5. Mom made beef __stew__ for dinner.

6. Mary __drew__ a picture of Mom.

7. Murphey likes to __chew__ on a bone.

8. Mom likes to wear __jewelry__.

9. The bird __flew__ high in the sky.

93

Answer Key

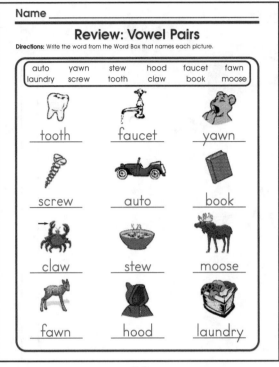

Review: Vowel Pairs

Directions: Write the word from the Word Box that names each picture.

| auto | yawn | stew | hood | faucet | fawn |
| laundry | screw | tooth | claw | book | moose |

tooth — faucet — yawn

screw — auto — book

claw — stew — moose

fawn — hood — laundry

94

The Sounds of Y

Directions: Read the words. Write each word in the correct column.

Sometimes **y** can sound like long **e**, and sometimes it can sound like long **i**.

puppy   fry

dry   baby   city   sky

pony   fly   bunny   cry

Y as Long e	Y as Long i
pony	dry
baby	sky
city	fly
bunny	cry

95

The Sounds of Y

Directions: Write the word from the Word Box that names each picture.

| bunny | fly | cry | money | muddy | city |
| puppy | sky | baby | fry | key | dry |

spy — muddy — fry

dry — key — sky

cry — city — money

baby — puppy — fly

96

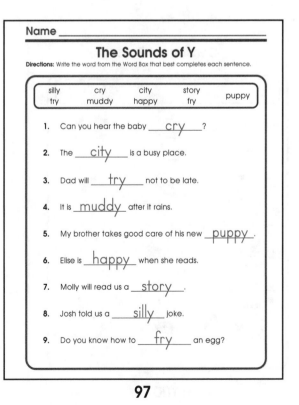

The Sounds of Y

Directions: Write the word from the Word Box that best completes each sentence.

| silly | cry | city | story | |
| try | muddy | happy | fry | puppy |

1. Can you hear the baby __cry__?

2. The __city__ is a busy place.

3. Dad will __try__ not to be late.

4. It is __muddy__ after it rains.

5. My brother takes good care of his new __puppy__.

6. Elise is __happy__ when she reads.

7. Molly will read us a __story__.

8. Josh told us a __silly__ joke.

9. Do you know how to __fry__ an egg?

97

Answer Key

Name _____

Check Up: Vowel Pairs and Sounds of Y
Directions: Write the name of each picture.

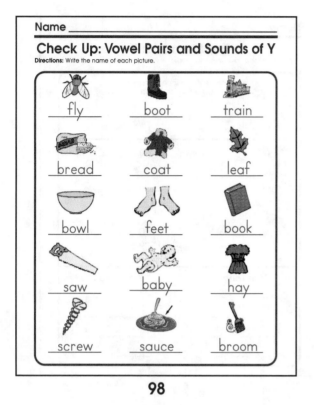

fly	boot	train
bread	coat	leaf
bowl	feet	book
saw	baby	hay
screw	sauce	broom

98

Name _____

Consonant Pairs
Directions: Write the letters **sh**, **ch**, **th**, or **wh** to complete each word. Then, write each word again.

1.	_sh_ op	shop
2.	_th_ read	thread
3.	_sh_ ell	shell
4.	_th_ ree	three
5.	_wh_ ale	whale
6.	_ch_ ain	chain
7.	_th_ in	thin
8.	_ch_ icks	chicks
9.	_wh_ eel	wheel
10.	_sh_ oe	shoe

99

Name _____

Consonant Pairs
Directions: Write the word from the Word Box that names each picture.

wheel	ship	chair	whale	shoe	shelf
think	cheese	throat	thread	cheek	thin

throat	think	ship
wheel	shoe	thin
whale	shelf	cheese
thread	chair	cheek

100

Name _____

Final Consonant Pairs
Directions: Write the final consonant pair **sh**, **ch**, **tch**, **th**, or **ng** to complete each word. Then, write each word again.

1.	ri_ng_	ring
2.	spri_ng_	spring
3.	di_sh_	dish
4.	bran_ch_	branch
5.	chur_ch_	church
6.	stri_ng_	string
7.	ba_th_	bath
8.	bru_sh_	brush
9.	wi_ng_	wing
10.	too_th_	tooth

101

Answer Key

Answer Key

Name _____

Final Consonant Pairs and Blends

Directions: Write the word that rhymes with each word below.

string	<u>ring</u>
wrench	<u>bench</u>
spring	<u>wing</u>
link	<u>sink</u>
path	<u>bath</u>

102

Name _____

Review: Consonant Pairs and Blends

Directions: Write the word from the Word Box that names each picture.

bench	wing	string	chain	watch	path
three	throne	whale	ship	ring	think

<u>wing</u>   <u>string</u>   <u>watch</u>

<u>think</u>   <u>path</u>   <u>ship</u>

<u>ring</u>   <u>whale</u>   <u>throne</u>

<u>chain</u>   <u>bench</u>   <u>three</u>

103

Name _____

Check Up: Consonant Pairs and Blends

Directions: Write the word or words from the Word Box that best completes each sentence.

wing	beach	chunk	bring	bench	cheese
shade	wash	path	ship	splash	shoes

1. The mouse ate a <u>chunk</u> of <u>cheese</u>.

2. Mom and Dad sailed on a <u>ship</u>.

3. Can you <u>bring</u> a snack to the picnic?

4. Patty walked on the <u>path</u> in the woods.

5. My sister is sitting on the green <u>bench</u> in the park.

6. To stay cool, I sit in the <u>shade</u>.

7. The bluebird has a broken <u>wing</u>.

8. At the <u>beach</u>, we like to <u>splash</u> in the water.

9. You should <u>wash</u> your dirty <u>shoes</u>.

104

Name _____

Vowels With R: AR and ER

Directions: Write the word from the Word Box that names each picture.

jar	barn	yarn	hammer	paper	letter
dart	ladder	slippers	fern	harp	star

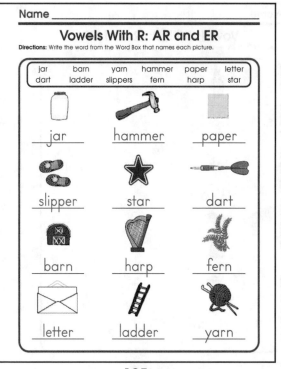

<u>jar</u>   <u>hammer</u>   <u>paper</u>

<u>slipper</u>   <u>star</u>   <u>dart</u>

<u>barn</u>   <u>harp</u>   <u>fern</u>

<u>letter</u>   <u>ladder</u>   <u>yarn</u>

105

Spectrum Phonics Grade 2

153

Answer Key

Answer Key

Name _____

Vowels With R: AR and ER
Directions: Write the missing letters **ar** or **er** for each word. Then, write each word again.

1. danc_er_   dancer
2. f_ar_m   farm
3. slipp_er_s   slippers
4. c_ar_   car
5. lett_er_   letter
6. y_ar_n   yarn
7. p_ar_k   park
8. camp_er_   camper
9. hamm_er_   hammer
10. st_ar_   star

106

Name _____

Vowels With R: IR and OR
Directions: Write the word from the Word Box that names each picture.

dirt	thorn	bird	girl	corn	fort
storm	cork	thirty	fork	shirt	skirt

cork   girl   corn

dirt   fork   storm

skirt   shirt   bird

thirty   thorn   fort

107

Name _____

Vowels With R: IR and OR
Directions: Write the missing letters **ir** or **or** for each word. Then, write each word again.

1. h_or_se   horse
2. sk_ir_t   skirt
3. f_or_k   fork
4. st_or_m   storm
5. g_ir_l   girl
6. c_or_n   corn
7. sh_ir_t   shirt
8. b_ir_d   bird
9. th_or_n   thorn
10. c_or_d   cord

108

Name _____

Vowels With R: UR
Directions: Write the word from the Word Box that names each picture.

hurt	fur	turn	burn	curb

turn   fur   burn

curb   hurt

Directions: Write two sentences. Use one word from above in each sentence.

1. _____
   _____

2. _____
   _____

Sentences will vary

109

Answer Key

Name _____

Vowels With R

Directions: Write the word that rhymes with each word below.

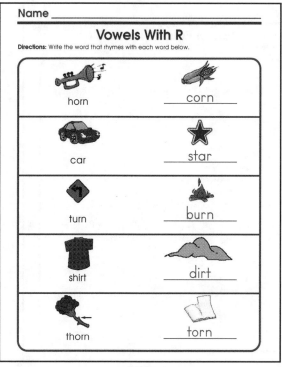

horn _____ <u>corn</u>

car _____ <u>star</u>

turn _____ <u>burn</u>

shirt _____ <u>dirt</u>

thorn _____ <u>torn</u>

110

Name _____

Vowels With R

Directions: Write the word from the Word Box that best completes each sentence.

| bird | fur | corn | fern | |
| cart | barn | hurt | bark | horn |

1. The bear's <u>fur</u> keeps it warm.

2. That <u>fern</u> is a very pretty plant.

3. Grandpa put the hay in the <u>barn</u>.

4. Grandma ate <u>corn</u> on the cob for dinner.

5. I <u>hurt</u> my foot playing soccer.

6. Fido will <u>bark</u> when he wants a bone.

7. The <u>cart</u> has four wheels.

8. I found a baby <u>bird</u> in its nest.

9. My sister plays the <u>horn</u> in the school band.

111

Name _____

Review: Vowels With R

Directions: Write the word from the Word Box that names each picture.

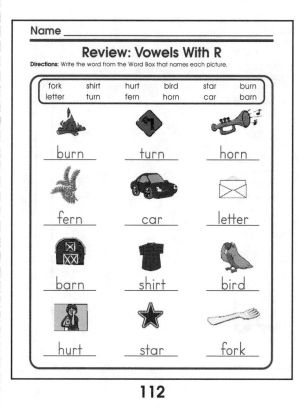

| fork | shirt | hurt | bird | star | burn |
| letter | turn | fern | horn | car | barn |

<u>burn</u>   <u>turn</u>   <u>horn</u>

<u>fern</u>   <u>car</u>   <u>letter</u>

<u>barn</u>   <u>shirt</u>   <u>bird</u>

<u>hurt</u>   <u>star</u>   <u>fork</u>

112

Name _____

Check Up: Vowels With R

Directions: Write six sentences. Use one word from the Word Box in each sentence.

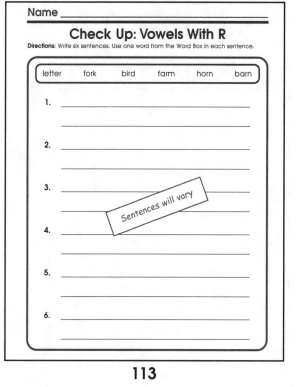

| letter | fork | bird | farm | horn | barn |

1. _____

2. _____

3. _____

Sentences will vary

4. _____

5. _____

6. _____

113

Answer Key

Answer Key

Name _____

Vowel Pairs: OI and OY

Directions: The vowel pairs **oi** and **oy** can make the sound that you hear in the middle of the words *noise* and *boys*. Write the word from the Word Box that names each picture.

| boil | boys | soil | coins | point | toys |

boys   soil   coins

point   boil   toys

Directions: Write two sentences. Use one word from above in each sentence.

1. _____

_____

2. _____   *Sentences will vary*

_____

114

Name _____

Vowel Pairs: OI and OY

Directions: Write the missing letters **oi** or **oy** for each word. Then, write the word again.

1. b_oi_l   boil
2. c_oi_ns   coins
3. b_oy_s   boys
4. s_oi_l   soil
5. _oy_ster   oyster
6. _oi_l   oil
7. t_oy_s   toys
8. p_oi_nt   point

115

Name _____

Vowel Pairs: OI and OY

Directions: Write the word from the Word Box that best completes each sentence.

| boys | voice | enjoys | noise | |
| soil | join | toys | coins | point |

1. Her loud __voice__ hurts my ears.
2. I broke the __point__ on my pencil.
3. How many __coins__ do you have in your pocket?
4. We gave the baby two new __toys__ to play with.
5. Our car is making a funny __noise__ .
6. Those __boys__ are friends from school.
7. Mark is going to __join__ the reading club.
8. We got the __soil__ ready so we could plant our garden.
9. Mom __enjoys__ going to the library.

116

Name _____

Vowel Pairs: OU and OW

Directions: The vowel pairs **ou** and **ow** can make the sound you hear in the middle of *mouth* and *clown*. Write the word from the Word Box that names each picture.

| shower | pound | plow | crown | house | clown |
| cow | blouse | flower | bounce | frown | gown |

gown   flower   clown

blouse   frown   cow

house   pound   crown

plow   bounce   shower

117

Answer Key

Name _____

Vowel Pairs: OU and OW
Directions: Write the missing letters **ou** or **ow** for each word. Then, write each word again.

1.		cl_OU_d	cloud
2.		m_OU_th	mouth
3.		_OW_l	owl
4.		cl_OW_n	clown
5.		p_OU_nd	pound
6.		pl_OW_	plow
7.		cr_OW_n	crown
8.		c_OW_	cow
9.		fl_OW_er	flower
10.		h_OU_se	house

118

Name _____

Vowel Pairs: OU and OW
Directions: Write the word from the Word Box that best completes each sentence.

cloud	mouse	clown	house	crown
blouse	ground	cow	pound	

1. The queen wears a gold __crown__ .

2. The little __mouse__ likes to nibble on cheese.

3. Dad uses the hammer to __pound__ nails.

4. The __clown__ did funny tricks.

5. Mom has a pretty blue __blouse__ and skirt.

6. The __cow__ likes to munch on grass.

7. There is a puffy white __cloud__ in the sky.

8. I dropped my watch on the __ground__ .

9. My __house__ is not far from school.

119

Name _____

Review: Vowel Pairs
Directions: Write the word that rhymes with each word below.

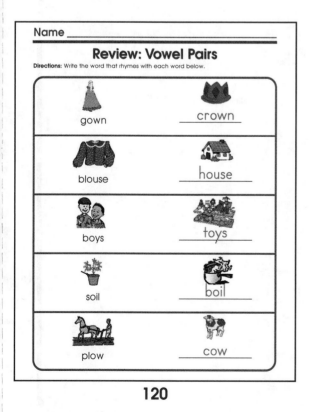

gown	crown
blouse	house
boys	toys
soil	boil
plow	cow

120

Name _____

Check Up: Vowel Pairs
Directions: Write a word that names each picture. Each word should have the **oi, oy, ou,** or **ow** vowel pair.

flower	soil	toys
pound	coins	cloud
boil	house	boys
oil	point	clown

121

Notes

Notes

Notes